MW01095094

The Mental Game of Athletic Administration

MASTERS OF THE MENTAL GAME SERIES BOOK

**Brian M. Cain, MS, CMAA
with Ethan Miller**

Brian Cain Peak Performance, LLC

WHAT CHAMPIONS ARE SAYING ABOUT BRIAN CAIN AND *THE MENTAL GAME OF ATHLETIC ADMINISTRATION*

"Brian Cain is the Master of the Mental Game. He has had a huge impact on how we run our athletic department, and was instrumental in helping us establish our core values and a process to help all coaches and athletes know what they are, what they look like in action and how to live and grow them in themselves and their programs."

Eric Davis
Athletic Director
Hanford High School
Richland, WA

"I wish I had read this book when I first started out as an AD. This would have saved me a TON of time and stress. This is a must-read for anyone who wants to get into athletic administration."

Mike O'Day
Athletic Director
South Burlington High School
South Burlington, VT
NIAAA Hall of Fame

"Brian Cain lived in the trenches for 7 years as an AD. He holds the CMAA designation from the NIAAA. He knows that it takes to excel as an AD. He lives it on a daily basis."

Kevin Ozee
Athletic Director
Arlington Independent School District, TX

"A classic that every AD should own."

Steve Millsaps, CAA
Athletic Director
West Joliet High School
Joliet, IL

"The Mental Game of Athletic Administration gives you the exact blueprint that Brian Cain uses when working with the top coaches and athletes in the country. He has worked with our coaches and athletes at Rowan. These principles work when you use them in athletics and in life."

Erin Barney
Asst. Athletic Director
Rowan University

"The strategies for success in *The Mental Game of Athletic Administration* will help you learn to better manage the monster that is the job of being an athletic director."

Chris Lavoie
Athletic Director
Celebration High School
Celebration, FL

"Brian Cain is a beast. He lives what he teaches you in this book."

Bob Wager
Athletic Coordinator
James Martin High School
Arlington, TX

"Being an athletic director presents challenges like no other position in education. If you are going to succeed at the highest level, you will need an elite mindset and a stronger administrative skill set. Cain shares with you in *The Mental Game of Athletic Administration* how to achieve both through simple sport psychology training."

Vince Brown
Athletic Director
Foothill High School
Tustin, CA

If this book has had a positive impact on the way you lead your athletic department and you would like to have a testimonial featured in future editions of *The Mental Game of Athletic Administration,* please e-mail your testimonial to admin@briancain.com.

We look forward to hearing how this book has positively affected your professional career and life. We would also welcome the opportunity of working with you to become a master of the mental game and to help you DOMINATE the day.

In Excellence,

Your Peak Performance Coach for Athletics Administration,

Brian M. Cain, MS, CMAA

The Mental Game of Athletic Administration

MASTERS OF THE MENTAL GAME SERIES BOOK

Brian M. Cain, MS, CMAA
with Ethan Miller

Brian Cain Peak Performance, LLC

Brian M. Cain, MS, CMAA with Ethan Miller
Peak Performance Publishing
Brian Cain Peak Performance, LLC

The Mental Game of Athletic Administration

A Masters of the Mental Game Series Book

©2016 by Brian M. Cain, MS, CMAA with Ethan Miller

Printed in the United States of America
Edited by: Mary Lou Schueler
Cover Design & Manual Layout: Brian M. Cain
Photography: Multiple Sources

Brian M. Cain, MS, CMAA with Ethan Miller
The Mental Game of Athletic Administration
A Masters of the Mental Game Series Book

ISBN-13: 978-1530198801
ISBN-10: 1530198801

PREFACE

Being an Athletic Administrator, or the commonly used title of Athletic Director (AD), can be a very exciting and rewarding occupation. You get to be around sports, working with coaches and athletes, while being the face of the department. These are just a few reasons why one chooses this career. Most who enter this career want to make a difference and care deeply for their school, coaches, and athletes. Those who have spent years within this career know that this position is not merely showing up and watching games (as every AD will hear someone say, 'That's great, you get to watch games for a living'). In seven years as an AD, I don't think I got to watch one game due to running around making sure the event came off smoothly.

There are numerous roles that Athletic Administrators must play in order to best serve their schools—fundraiser, sports information director, strength and conditioning coach, athletic trainer, sport psychologist and public relations consultant are only a few of the hats you wear as an AD. You must also handle parent issues, academic eligibility, budgets, scheduling, personnel decisions and discipline. The turnover rate in this position is alarming, often due to the burnout and stress AD's experience in the office and in their own personal lives.

Athletic Administrators must have a collection of tools at their disposal to successfully meet the demands that the position calls for. Many Athletic Administrators today are former coaches and teachers who have had very little formal training in administration, leadership, and helping coaches and athletes create a process to be at their best. As a former AD myself, I know the commitment this position demands to even be average, let alone excellent.

This book is an extensive collection of my experiences working as an AD for seven years and now as a Peak Performance Coach and Sport Psychology Consultant with some of the top college and high school programs in the country.

I have worked with Athletic Administrators who successfully built a Championship Culture and made the most out of their day with clear intent and purpose, and with those who had great intentions and fell short of their goals. This book is a body of work that, when put into action, will unlock your potential and take you to the next level.

This is a book about the process of **becoming a person and a program of excellence**.

This is a book on **strategies for success** in athletic administration.

This is a book about **becoming a champion** so that you can win more championships.

This is a book designed for those who want more and know that you must **become more** so that you can get more out of yourself and others.

This book will provide you with the guiding principles that will give you the best chance for success in athletic administration and in life.

The material in this book has worked for real Athletic Administrators in real college and high school programs around the country. I have been with them along the way to experience the highs and the lows. There are always plenty of lows when you are the one leading from the front and making decisions for what you feel is best for the institution you represent.

This is not a book on theory; it is a book on APPLICATION!

Whether you are a veteran of athletic administration or just getting started, this book will provide insight and information you can use IMMEDIATELY to start becoming your best and creating masters of the mental game.

DOMINATE THE DAY!

DEDICATION

This book is dedicated to all of the Athletic Administrators out there who realize the value of athletics, teamwork, leadership and peak performance.

This book is dedicated to you, the reader, because you are taking a step to become more. If you want to become more, you must have two critical pieces of the puzzle:

1. You must have a coach.

2. You must have an accountability partner.

I hope this book serves in those two capacities for you.

You have chosen to invest the time it takes to be different, abnormal and uncommon, in order to take your leadership and life to the next level. You want more, and my mission through this book is to help you establish a process so that you can become more.

By signing your name below, you are dedicating yourself to reading and, more importantly, to applying this book and making the commitment to enjoy the journey to the summit of The Mountain of Athletic Administrative Excellence.

I _____ (print your name) have been given everything I need to become an AD of excellence.

I am fully capable of living the life of my dreams, and leaving this world and those I serve better than when I got here.

I am a TRUE daily dominator who lives and competes in the present and chooses to focus on the process over the outcome, and I will stay positive in the face of adversity.

ACKNOWLEDGMENTS

It is with sincere and deep appreciation that I, Brian M. Cain, acknowledge the support and guidance of all the Athletic Administrators who have given me inside access into their programs, families, lives and experiences that have made me the person I am today.

There are so many people to thank that there are not enough pages in this book. I apologize ahead of time if you don't see your name here and are offended. Unfortunately, I know that will happen and you will call me on it. I can't wait...

I want to give special thanks to Dr. Ken Ravizza, my mentor at Cal State Fullerton and the man who taught me most of the strategy and philosophy shared in these pages.

I also want to thank the best AD who ever lived, Mike O'Day, for taking me under his wing and showing me what excellence looks like. I would also like to thank Kevin Ozee and Eric Davis for demonstrating a high level of commitment to the mental game and for leading with the process in mind.

I, Ethan Miller, have many thanks to give out for I feel like I am standing on the shoulders of giants. I am where I am and who I am today because of those who have come before me and helped pave the way for my life; for that I am forever grateful.

To my family, teachers, coaches, teammates, colleagues and friends who are too many to mention here yet have all inspired me to become more each and every day. I have been blessed beyond measure to be associated with so many positive influences.

I am thankful for my wife Becky who has provided the support needed in order for me to perform my job as AD at the highest level and to attack this life together - you are the ultimate Accountability Partner.

Lastly to Brian Cain who in August 2015 set my life into a direction that I had wanted to go and for providing the methods and tools necessary to get there.

CONTENTS

AUTHOR'S NOTE

The intent of the author in writing this book in The Masters of the Mental Game Series was to create a comprehensive training program that could be used by Athletic Administrators as their blueprint for mastering the mental game.

The mental game is about searching within yourself to see what you are made of as a person. When you search within yourself, you learn that all the answers to life's questions and challenges live inside you. As you work your way through this book, you will learn what drives you by continuously reflecting upon your attitudes and actions.

While reading this book, you will recognize the mental adjustments and changes you must make to access all the untapped and limitless potential that resides inside you. Tapping into every ounce of combined mental and physical potential is the art of peak performers, and the book will teach you this art form by teaching you to search from within.

This photo has impacted me since I first saw it in 2002 in a graduate school philosophy class with Dr. Ken Ravizza.

For me, this picture illustratively captures the concept of one's ability to search within oneself for the answers to life's questions.

My life's mission is to help you uncover the excellence that lies within you, and to serve as your coach as you develop the tools necessary to achieve your best as an AD and in life by taking a look inside and always maximizing the day that you have been given.

Don't count the days you have had on the job as an AD or the days you have left, make the days count.

INTRODUCTION

INTRODUCTION TO THE MENTAL GAME OF ATHLETIC ADMINISTRATION

> "We cannot become what we need to be, remaining what we are."
>
> *Max Depree*
> *American Businessman & Writer*

What is peak performance in athletic administration? What does it mean to give yourself the best chance for success and to be your best when it means the most?

What is mental conditioning and why is it essential to both understanding and answering those two questions?

This is your mental conditioning program for athletic administration, a 10-chapter/10-week training program that will give you the knowledge and techniques to unlock all of your performance potential within your athletic department.

The professional athletes, Olympic champions, collegiate national champions, and high school state championship-winning programs I have worked with have all experienced one thing in common: *As they elevate to higher levels of competition, success becomes less about the physical skills and more about the mental game.*

This truth is essential to acknowledging and appreciating the importance of mental conditioning. The more you think about it, the more obvious it becomes. At the highest levels of competition, everyone has the physical skills to be successful, or they would not be competing at that level. Talent is just not enough. If it were, every 1st round pick in the Major League Baseball Draft would make it to the Major Leagues, but less than half of them ever do.

Thus, on top of developing the physical skills to compete at the highest level, coaches and athletes must devote more time to the development of their mental game that will allow them to perform consistently at their best.

To further emphasize the importance of mastering the mental game, there is a simple two-word sentence to convey the significance of mental conditioning as it relates to athletics: ***Consistency wins.***

CONSISTENCY IN EACH DAY

Consistency is the significant difference between the good and the great administrators, coaches, players and teams. Those who compete at the highest level on a consistent basis are the legendary and iconic figures in the game like Derek Jeter, Wayne Gretzky, Michael Jordan, and Joe Montana. Then there are those who are great leaders, such as John Wooden, Dan Gable and Vince Lombardi.

Consistency is crucial to performing at a high level. This begins with your work ethic, as you must have the burning desire to compete and win so that you will do the things necessary to put yourself in a position to succeed, which will then lead to the success of your program.

As we will explore throughout this book, your daily routines will give you the best chance to lock in on each day and lead with a relentless focus. Being an effective leader is not about one act, but a series of decisions repeated daily. We call this *The Compound Effect.* The consistency you will find will not only make you a better leader, but a better husband, wife, father or mother, whatever title you bear that carries great responsibility.

A good indicator that you are becoming a master of the mental game is to become aware that your laser-like focus is the same every day, regardless of what you did in the past or what you are going to do in your future.

Hall of Fame pitcher Tom Seaver said: *"In baseball, my theory is to strive for consistency, not to worry about the numbers. If you dwell on statistics you get shortsighted; if you aim for consistency, the numbers will be there at the end."* A consistent focus on the process, putting together quality days and executing quality decisions, will give you your best chance to have success.

Anyone who holds the position of Athletic Administrator has the skills necessary to perform at the highest levels of his/her ability once in a while, but it is the TRUE daily dominator who stands out among everyone else – the one who brings their best every day and every time he or she steps on campus. That's the person who will make the biggest impact on their team, in their school, and who will ultimately have the greatest career.

> "Excellence is not a skill. It is an attitude."
>
> **Ralph Marston**
> **Creator of The Daily Motivator**

WHAT MAKES THE BEST OF THE BEST

Every Athletic Administrator wants high levels of success for the programs they lead. To better understand what can be done within your own school, you must understand what others have done and the success that follows. When at the games watching teams compete and performing as game day manager, we often revel in the physical characteristics of the athletes on hand. Physical development is crucial and the coaches on staff are working to better all of the athletes.

The most competitive athletes and programs invest significant amounts of time and energy into the many grueling hours it takes to train their bodies for performance at the highest levels.

Derek Jeter once said, *"There may be people that have more talent than you, but there's no excuse for anyone to work harder than you do."*

Successful programs are well organized in everything they do. If you have ever seen video clips of Coach Nick Saban's practices at the University of Alabama, you see first and foremost the attention to detail taken during the individual segments and how that morphs to create the entire practice. Every drill, every segment, every practice, and every meeting has substantial impact on the players and getting them to compete physically at a championship level.

MENTAL CONDITIONING IS ESSENTIAL

The greatest players and teams in athletics are aware of something that you might not realize: *If you want to be the best of the best, doing the physical training is simply not enough.*

Dave Serrano, current head baseball coach at the University of Tennessee and former national championship-winning pitching coach at Cal State Fullerton (2004), told me once that belief in the mental game is what separates good programs from the great ones.

Serrano said this about his 2004 National Champion squad: *"I think that the Cal State Fullerton National Championship team in 2004 was not the most talented team in the country, but we were the most mentally prepared team that year. The mental preparation that goes into getting ready for a practice, a game or a season is the same type of preparation that these athletes will have to do when they are done playing and are out working in the real world. Like in baseball, in the real world success often finds the one who has prepared the most."*

Champions know that mental conditioning is essential in order to develop a psychological edge over their greatest competitors and give them the confidence to compete at a high level.

The greatest competitors understand that peak performance occurs only when the body and the mind are working together to maximize their performance potential. Your greatest performances to this day have come when your psychology and physiology are aligned. Thus, the best of the best know that mental conditioning is as vital to their success as physical conditioning.

THE POWER OF THE MIND

The power of the mind is as miraculous as it is incomprehensible. Studies have continued for years, and we are still miles away from truly understanding the full capabilities of the human brain. Countless examples of the "mind over matter" type of experience have been documented over time.
There are incredible examples of prisoners of war being released and performing amazing physical feats that they had practiced mentally

during their detentions.

One such example is of a POW who came out of exile having visualized playing golf every day. By the time he was free and stepped onto a golf course, he lowered his golf game by ten strokes. Upon his release, another POW who practiced mental conditioning became a competent guitarist by teaching himself the guitar through repetitive visualization processes, despite only having played the instrument minimally before.

There are endless miraculous stories similar to these, and it is safe to say that, even though neurological function is not as well-understood as the physiological, no one is prepared to discount the human mind as the most powerful tool available in the world.

The good news is that, even without understanding the scientific intricacies of the human mind, anyone can improve their mental toughness for athletics with a simple mental conditioning program and by doing simple exercises on a routine basis. You learn best in conditioning yourself to be the toughest mentally just like you do physically – by *doing a little a lot, not a lot a little.*

MENTAL CONDITIONING FOR ATHLETICS

Mental conditioning for athletics is the process of developing mental toughness, by which an individual exercises and develops the awareness to control his mental state in order to control his behavior. My mentor Dr. Ken Ravizza taught his students that *you must be in control of yourself before you can control your performance on the field* – and gaining self-control in the field of sport is essential to an athlete's success. *Gaining self-control is largely related to your ability to take a breath pre-play and to manage the voice inside your head.*

In dividing the two words, **mental** relates to the mind, while conditioning means to train oneself to behave in a certain way or to accept certain circumstances that will happen in a game, such as an umpire missing a call, the other team putting together a time consuming drive or having to move on to the next play after committing a turnover. Mental conditioning is a process similar to how you would physically condition your body in the weight room.

When you lift weights infrequently, you don't get any stronger; but when you lift weights consistently, the timely repetition will make you stronger. Mental toughness is developed the same way, by doing a little a lot.

Mental conditioning gives you the techniques to develop control over the beliefs in your mind. Beliefs (both positive and negative) shape our behavior, create our experiences and determine our results.

THE POWER OF BELIEFS

Philosophers and spiritual leaders have been preaching the power of beliefs for centuries, while scientists have been conducting research on how the mind works for decades. Pioneers in sport psychology – such as Dr. Ken Ravizza and Harvey Dorfman – were among the first in our culture to recognize the practical application of positive affirmation training, visualization and the implications of mental conditioning for their performance. So many of the limits in our life are put there by our own thoughts and imagination, and can be removed and destroyed with proper mental conditioning.

The best coaches now understand that they can dramatically improve their players' confidence, resilience and attitude in the face of adversity, and their on-field performance reliability, by integrating positive confidence conditioning statements and mental imagery into their daily training regimens.

Peak performance and success strategist Tony Robbins says, *"Beliefs have the power to create and the power to destroy."* Many of your beliefs are not decided consciously but are formed based on previous experiences you've had. If these beliefs do not get you excited about your life and the future ahead of you, you must begin conditioning your mind and body with beliefs that support you in your pursuit of excellence.

The goal of this book is to give you the tools to develop your mental game, shatter limiting beliefs, develop the confidence and consistency needed to lead your departments, and give yourself the best chance to win on the scoreboard and, more importantly, in life.

CAIN'S COACHING POINT:
The mental conditioning skills you will learn to perform at

your best in your role as administrator will also help you to perform at your best in life. Great leaders recognize this and realize the important duty they have to train young people to be successful in life through athletics.

COACHES' BUILT-IN EXCUSE:
NOT HAVING A MENTAL CONDITIONING SYSTEM

It is an unfortunate reality that many athletic programs leave mental toughness to chance. Many coaches think that their players will either figure it out or they won't – that their players either 'have it together between the ears' or they do not. Many coaches think players are born mentally tough or mentally weak. This old-school thinking is actually an excuse for not knowing how to train and develop mental toughness in their athletes.

These coaches believe there is nothing they as coaches can do to help enhance the athlete's mental toughness other than tough physical conditioning, and yet they will agree that performing at your best when it means the most is as much about the six inches between your ears as it is about the six feet below them.

This coaching mentality fails to recognize that developing a strong mental game has just as much, if not more, significant value to performance than developing a strong physical game.

EXCUSE EXTERMINATOR IN YOUR HANDS

Until now, mental toughness training for Athletic Administrators has been largely left to chance. Many athletic programs have not made the investment of bringing in a peak performance coach or researching the best strategies for training mindset, character and leadership skills. The number one excuse is that "there isn't enough time".

There will be a common theme throughout this book – you only have 86,400 seconds in a day and it is up to you to use them wisely. The top Athletic Administrators in the world know the clock is moving. The best have a plan in place to make their day work FOR them instead of their working FOR the day.

In this book, you will learn the importance of focusing on the **present moment,** and will gain a true understanding of what it means to have a **process-over-outcome** approach, a **positive attitude** and **how to develop a Championship Culture** that will be the fuel for all decisions and set the standard for coach and athlete behavior. No longer will you be a paper pusher and stressed to the max, but rather a heat-seeking missile putting into action the mission of your department to have the greatest positive impact you can on the coaches and athletes you lead.

MENTAL TOUGHNESS IS A SKILL SET

Mental toughness is simply a skill set that can be taught, developed and continuously improved, just like the physical aspect of athletics.

Mental conditioning is strength and conditioning for the six inches between your ears that control the six feet below them. Having a mental conditioning system is essential to helping your teams compete at their best when it means the most, **one play at a time** and **giving them the best chance for success.** Mental conditioning will give you a skill set to be successful in your role of Athletic Administrator, as well as that in your personal life. This is not your run-of-the-mill self-help strategy, this is a lifestyle choice that will allow you to take ownership of all things in your life.

THE 90%/10% SHIFT

Whether or not coaches and athletes understand the complete significance of mental conditioning, most coaches and athletes I have worked with would agree that training for competition is 90% physical and 10% mental. They acknowledge that a noticeable shift occurs when the first play takes place. In the heat of competition, they acknowledge that performance becomes 90% mental and 10% physical. This is called the 90%/10% shift to give athletes and coaches an illustrative taste of how valuable mental conditioning is when it is time to put the uniform on and compete.

The reality is that there should be no shift. Mental conditioning should be integrated into physical conditioning and every aspect of your athletes' preparation. It should be 100% mental and physical conditioning combined – one is never complete without the other.

@BrianCainPeak

This book will give you a system for training your mental game and for unlocking your true potential. As you read this book and develop your mental toughness, think about it as going to the gym to do strength and conditioning for your brain instead of your body. This book is your "Mind Gym."

CAIN'S BLUEPRINT FOR EXCELLENCE

I always get the question, "Brian, when you work with the top athletic programs, what do you teach?"

What I teach them is the same mental conditioning program that you will learn – about exactly how to be your best when it means the most, by teaching you how to:

- Live in the present moment and compete one day at a time.

- Act differently than how you feel and start having good and "bad" days.

- Focus on the process over the outcome.

- Identify what you can control and what you cannot.

- Have your own personal and program philosophy and core values.

- Challenge your limiting beliefs and your perspective.

- Stay positive in the face of adversity – and athletic administration is about handling that adversity.

- Help develop preparation and performance routines for consistent high-level athletic performance.

- Take responsibility for your performance and life.

- Relax, recover, and gain control of your thoughts, feelings, and emotions in life.

- Recognize your signal lights and develop the awareness to win the day.

- Release negative thoughts and refocus when you get distracted and when adversity hits.

- Use mental imagery to help you prepare and be more confident for the next situation.

- Inspire, lead and motivate yourself to make the impossible possible.

- Develop the dedication and self-discipline that you need to power through the grind it takes to succeed.

- Take action steps to make excellence a lifestyle, not an event.

These are the fundamentals of mental toughness, and they represent the blueprint I use when working with an athletic department to develop Personal Responsibility In Daily Excellence (PRIDE).

THE GOAL OF THE BOOK IN YOUR HANDS

The goal of the book in your hands is that you learn how to thrive in your position as Athletic Administrator so you can successfully lead others to achieve the level of athletic and life performance necessary to become a champion.

CAIN'S COACHING POINT:
If you want to win a championship, you must first become a champion. Using the skills taught in this book will make you a champion in the office and in life.

Everyone wants more – more from themselves, their coaches, their schools. If you want more, you must become more, and this book will give you a process to become more.

ONE DAY AT A TIME:
10-WEEK MENTAL CONDITIONING PROGRAM
FOR ATHLETIC ADMINISTRATORS

This book is written in a 10-week program format for thriving as an athletic administrator. By reading a chapter a week, you will grow into the AD you want to be.

We will focus on two critical principles of success:

1. Living one day at a time with clear intent and purpose.

2. Developing PRIDE – Personal Responsibility In Daily Excellence.

The PRIDE acronym serves as the backbone of this mental game system, reminding you of the significance of making excellence a daily pursuit for which you are personally responsible and accountable.

The outcome goal is that you become a peak performer as Athletic Administrator and in life. Before you can become a peak performer, you must first understand that excellence is a lifestyle, not an event, and is defined as being at your best when it means the most, which is every day.

CAIN'S COACHING POINT:
Excellence is being at your best when it means the most – every moment within every day.

For an Athletic Administrator, being your best when it means the most is dictated by how you plan your work and then work your plan. It is every email written. Every meeting you attend. Every class. Being an active participant in your own life. As legendary football coach Vince Lombardi said, *"The quality of a person's life is in direct proportion to their commitment to excellence, regardless of their chosen field of endeavor."*

Taking PRIDE is having an overall system for success and ***being able to describe what you do as a process so that you can be consistent over time.***

CLIMBING THE MOUNTAIN OF EXCELLENCE

Climbing the Mountain of Excellence is a symbolic concept used throughout this book. The summit of the mountain represents your goal, the mountain represents the obstacle you must conquer to reach it. The journey up the Mountain of Excellence marks the self-improvement endeavor an individual must take to become a peak performer.

CAIN'S COACHING POINT:
If you want more success on the field, you must become more off the field. Winning a championship is a by-product of becoming a champion.

This book employs the concept of the Mountain of Excellence to demonstrate that the achievement of performance excellence is a long but worthwhile journey.

Similar to mountain climbing, athletics are about training to conquer one mountain at a time. Once that mountain has been climbed, it is time to return to base camp and set your sights on the next mountain's summit and get to work. Each mountain is scaled one step at a time. It does not matter if you are climbing Mt. Everest, Mt. Greylock or the local hill in your town – all mountains are summited one step at a time, and all games are won one play at a time. Base camp is your office, meeting rooms, and facilities.

ONE STEP TO THE SUMMIT – STAY & YOU DIE

Mountain climbing also serves as a great activity to compare with athletics because when a team scales a mountain, they cannot simply live on the summit: they must return to base camp, regroup and climb another mountain, or their climbing career is over. Similarly, in athletics, an individual or team cannot win a championship and be champions forever. They will forever be champions of that season, but as soon as the next season rolls around, the slate is swept clean and all of the opposition is ready to become title contenders. This forces the champions to start the season anew in their quest for that season's championship, that climb's summit. Therefore, your time at the summit is only temporary.

Legendary LSU head baseball coach and athletic director Skip Bertman took the Tigers to the College World Series 11 times in 18 seasons, winning 5 national championships.

Bertman clearly understood that you can't live on the summit in Omaha. You must get back on the horse and ride or you will die. I had the great opportunity to work with Skip on writing the book *Winning the Big One: Motivation and Teamwork You Can Use* and the accompanying DVD and CD. This is a MUST for ADs. Check it out at BrianCain.com/Products.

CAIN'S COACHING POINT:
It's key that you give yourself a certain time frame to enjoy successes or lick your wounds from failures. Giving both a deadline where you re-engage back into the moment gives you the best chance to prepare and perform consistently at your best. Some call this the "midnight rule" and force themselves to move on when the clock strikes midnight.

Ultimately, there is no end to the pursuit of excellence, no one final summit to reach. Excellence is a constant journey that demands personal responsibility in your daily commitment. As you read this book, the use of the mountain climbing analogy will assist your understanding and application of the mental game as you strive to become more.

WHAT'S YOUR SUMMIT?

In reading this book, it is clear that your immediate Mountain of Excellence is conquering this book to understand how to transform yourself into a peak performer and achieve performance excellence – to consistently be the best version of yourself. However, it is only by fully understanding the reasons for embarking on this journey and openly recognizing the larger mountain you desire to conquer that you will make the most of your personal growth and mental conditioning experience. Therefore, you must **begin with the end in mind** to give your journey a greater sense of purpose. You must know precisely where it is you want to end up and **why** you want to end up there, or you might find yourself climbing the wrong mountain – a mountain that someone else wanted you to climb, not the mountain you wanted to climb.

Think about your desired destination. Is it being inducted into your state AD Hall of Fame? Do you want your programs to win state or national championships? Do you want to become better at dealing with difficult parents? Become more efficient in how you operate each day? Whatever your journey, you must begin with the end in mind. You must have an outcome goal and a destination to start your journey.

CAIN'S COACHING POINT:
What is the Mountain of Excellence you desire to climb and conquer? What is it you want to accomplish?

_____

_____

_____

CAIN'S COACHING POINT:

Remember, you are allowed to climb more than one mountain, but should focus on one summit at a time. Keeping your mind in the present moment, sticking with the process and staying positive will help you to better enjoy your journey and experience more success than if you mountain-hop and pursue different summits during the day. Whatever mountain you are climbing at that time, focus on that specific summit. Be where you need to be when you need to be there, hike one step at a time, and live life one day at time.

"It is often said that the journey far outweighs the outcome. The championships are great – don't get me wrong. But it is another set of "ships" – relationships – that endure and last. That is what sport is all about – relationships, learning and giving it everything you have to become your very best you are capable of becoming."

Skip Bertman
Former LSU Baseball Head Coach & Athletic Director
5-Time NCAA National Champion

THREE STEPS TO ACCOMPLISHING ANYTHING

Most people have heard the saying "You can do anything if you set your mind to it," but are skeptical of deeming it a universal truth. Well, I am one of those people who believe that if you truly desire something, why not set your mind to it and give everything you've got to achieve it? To make your dreams become a reality, you must pursue your goals in an effective and realistic manner. This is why peak performers must understand and effectively utilize the three-step process to accomplishing anything, both in athletic administration and in life.

The three steps that give you the best chance to accomplish anything are these:

1. Make a commitment to your goal by writing it down and putting it where you can see it on a daily basis.

2. Make it public and share your goal with your coaching staff, friends, family, accountability partners and the people in your inner circle.

3. Work with a relentlessly positive energy on a daily basis to make it happen – the type of relentlessly positive energy that can only be found when you are pursuing something you are passionate about and have a reason why. So be very selective about your goals.

These three steps provide you with the strategy that gives you the best opportunity to accomplish anything you desire.

As you proceed on your journey through this book, utilize these steps to accomplish your process-based goals along the way. This is why you identified and established your mountain in the previous section – to facilitate the first step of this process in your personal journey. It is your job to facilitate step number two, and it is the purpose of this book to provide the information and knowledge to facilitate step number three so that you may conquer the mountain and reach its summit.

ONE DAY (TODAY) AT A TIME

Now that you have established your mountain and know the three principal steps to reaching the summit, it may still appear to be an intimidating mountain to climb. Do not be daunted by your destination. You chose it because you want it – because a fiery passion within you burns and yearns to shed its light on the snow-capped pinnacle of your mountain. You will conquer your Mountain of Excellence; it all comes down to taking the first step and then another and another until you reach the top. Have patience in the process and enjoy the journey.

INTRODUCTION REVIEW

- In athletics and in life, consistency wins.

- If you want your teams to be the best of the best, doing the physical conditioning is not enough. You must do both physical and mental conditioning.

- Peak performance occurs only when the body and the mind are working together to maximize their performance potential.

- The power of the mind is as miraculous as it is incomprehensible.

- Mental conditioning is the process of developing the mental toughness skill set by which an individual exercises and develops influence over his mental state in order to control his physical behavior.

- Mental toughness is taught, developed and continuously improved upon, just like going to the weight room for your physical toughness.

- Mental conditioning should be integrated into physical conditioning and every aspect of athletic performance. You do not separate the mental and physical conditioning; you do them together.

- Each day must be attacked with clear intent and purpose.

- PRIDE = Personal Responsibility In Daily Excellence

- Excellence is being at your best when it means the most – every single day.

- The Mountain of Excellence represents the obstacle you must conquer to reach your outcome goal at the summit.

- The journey up the Mountain of Excellence is a self-transformative endeavor an individual must take to become a peak performer.

- One cannot live at the summit; you have to keep hiking or you will die.

- There is no end to the pursuit of excellence. You never reach excellence; you are always in pursuit. Excellence is a lifestyle, not an event.

- Peak performance is a constant journey, pursuing excellence and demanding personal responsibility in this daily pursuit.

- Choose your Mountain of Excellence you desire to climb and conquer.

- Remember, you are allowed to climb more than one mountain, but should focus on one summit at a time.

CHAPTER #1

TAKING PRIDE IN LEADERSHIP AND EMBRACING THE JOURNEY AHEAD

> "It is not the mountain we conquer, but ourselves."
>
> ***Sir Edmund Hillary***
> ***Famed Mountain Climber & Philanthropist***

RISE AND GRIND

It's 5:30 am, the alarm clock is buzzing and you want to hit the snooze. You hosted a volleyball match last night that went 5 games and had all sorts of issues to make the night less than ideal. The fire alarm sounded before first serve because the volunteer in the concession stand burned the popcorn. Your ticket takers ran out of one dollar bills...twice. One of your line judges texted you an hour before start time indicating they were sick, and you were scrambling to find a replacement.

To make matters even more interesting, you had some complaining parents who were feeding off one another because their team isn't winning, and they feel their daughter should be playing more and they want a meeting first thing this morning. Sound familiar? Welcome to the world of the Athletic Administrator.

Every morning when you rise, there is a new set of challenges waiting at your office doorstep. Oh, did I mention that you have to teach a couple of classes, and then handle eligibility, then hand out the discipline from the party that got busted this past weekend? This is all too familiar, and makes one wonder why anybody in their right mind would enter into this profession. But here is the kicker: you are reading this because you don't want to just manage, you want to LEAD.

You want more out of yourself and out of your programs. You have pride in what you do and are searching for the best way to achieve it. This book is going to help you in your quest for excellence.

Each morning when you wake up, a new climb up the Mountain of Excellence begins. Every day it is time to rise and grind. In your backpack are your experiences and what you have learned on previous journeys from past days. You have to make your most important decision the split second your eyes crack – *am I going to take control of my day or allow my day to take control of me?*

The importance of taking one day at a time cannot be overstated. The school year covers a rather long period of time, so the focus must be on dominating the present moment with focus on the next 200 feet. You know your desired destination – the summit of your mountain – but you must familiarize and condition yourself with the fundamental principles necessary not just to survive but to thrive.

This must be done on a daily basis. Start by breaking the journey down into smaller chunks – fall sports, winter sports, spring sports, and summer sports, camps, activities. We will dive into this further in the next chapter, but know right now that the mindset you have in thinking small is a step in the right direction to having something big. It will be a challenge but it will be worth it. *It is the start that stops most people, and the start of your day is the most important part of your day.*

As any mountain climber preparing to ascend Mount Everest can attest, one must gradually build the stamina and conditioning for the long trek to the summit. Putting in the time and establishing mental endurance is of high importance, so that you are prepared for the treacherous conditions you are bound to face on your long journey. *Embrace the adversity* and practice the mindset you need to succeed one day at a time to reach your summit.

WHAT DOES LEADERSHIP MEAN TO YOU?

You demand more of yourself and want to get the most out of your potential and that of your school and athletic programs. You are the one at the front of the pack leading the way. There are many different leadership styles and you must decide which is going to work best for you. However, you must keep in mind that the goal here must be function over feeling. What is going to allow you to accomplish your goals while maintaining who you are as a person?

LEADER VS. MANAGER

We have often heard the terms *leadership* and *management* used interchangeably. The general consensus was that "they are one and the same." However, they are different. Most people now recognize that there is a significant difference between the two.

Management is at its best when things stay the same. Sports fans often hear the term in a negative light when used to characterize a quarterback in football: "game manager." Managers make sure that everyone is doing their job and keeping the status quo.

Leadership deals with people and their dynamics, which are continually changing. Leadership is taking a situation and inspiring others to be better than they thought they could be. The leaders are the ones with propellers in their heads who consistently examine their craft and how it can improve. **They inspect what they expect.**

There are fundamental characteristics that set leaders apart from managers:

1. Managers are about stability and maintenance, while leaders are about growth and change.

2. Managers make the rules, while leaders adapt and adjust for the sake of them.

3. Managers plan details, while leaders set the direction of where the team is going.

4. Managers execute culture, while leaders create and shape the culture.

5. Managers try to avoid conflict, while leaders use conflict as an asset because they understand that there is no progress without friction.

6. Managers use existing roads where things are comfortable, while leaders create new roads and become comfortable with being uncomfortable.

7. Managers tend to take credit, while leaders are selfless and give the credit to the team for helping them succeed.

8. Managers make the decisions, while leaders support decisions by encouraging and listening to everyone's voice.

9. Managers tell, and leaders sell. They sell the vision and direction they are going with enthusiasm because they know the last four letters of enthusiasm stand for **I am sold myself.**

10. Managers are transactions; what are the transactions to get something from someone? A leader is transformational, transforming the team members that he/she leads into becoming more.

11. Management is doing things right. Leadership is doing the right things.

12. Managers manage people and things. Leaders develop followers by being the examples others want to emulate.

The problem with management is that people do not respond as well to being managed and told what to do as they once did. Micromanaging is not a leadership style; it's more of a leadership failure. People do not want to be managed. They want to be led. They want their leaders to treat them like they are part of a team and allow them to feel as if they have a part ownership of the process.

> "Leadership is not about titles, positions, or flowcharts. It is about one life influencing another."
>
> *John C. Maxwell*
> *Author & Leadership Expert*

GETTING YOUR HANDS DIRTY

When it comes to leadership styles, I'm reminded of a story that a friend of mine told when he made money in the summer working construction. The company he worked for while in college was formed by a man in his late 80s who had long since retired and handed the business over to his sons.

One hot July day while erecting a building that would house a small town fire department, the sons who now owned and operated the business came by to check on the progress. The two sons questioned the foreman on a few of his decisions. The foreman had been with the company for 40 years and knew every in and out of how construction worked. He answered their questions calmly and the sons were on their way.

After the exchange, the foreman told my friend, "You would have loved the original owner." When my friend asked him why he responded, "He made you feel like you were a part of something. After he got into the managerial and ownership aspect at a later age, he still traveled around once a week to put in a day's work with the crews. He wanted to feel the dirt between his fingers with those who busted their butts for him and his company. His sons have never felt the dirt between their fingers, let alone underneath their nails."

This is an incredible story of getting down and doing the dirty work with those whom you want to lead. Many, if not all of us, started with a background in teaching and coaching before moving in to the position of Athletic Administrator. Too often we have those within the profession who forgot what those days were like and become a different type of leader, and have a negative influence upon their audience. Lead from the front and pull the weight together in the direction towards the vision, not screaming commands from the back as they do all the work moving the load.

CAIN'S COACHING POINT:
Reflect upon your own leadership style and tendencies.

_____

_____

_____

What leadership style does this fall into? Is this an effective way for you to attain the goals you have set for your athletic department?

_____

_____

_____

LEADERSHIP STARTS WITH YOU

Before you can attempt to lead people into a new direction, you have to be willing to take yourself into a new direction. One thing that people today do not utilize enough is that of self-assessment. This exercise starts the process of looking inward before outward.

What are 3 of your strengths?

1. _____

2. _____

3. _____

What are 3 of your weaknesses?

1. _____

2. _____

3. _____

This very simple set of questions, if done honestly, will lend your mind and heart to focus on those characteristics that make you who you are at this moment in your life. We are all in the process of self-discovery and self-improvement and helping bridge the gap from where you are to where you want to be.

By assessing yourself and the love/hate we have with our habits that comprise all who you are, we understand that **we must be in total control of ourselves before we can attempt to help impact and influence others.**

WHAT ARE YOUR INDIVIDUAL CORE VALUES?

As you set your sights on the summit of The Mountain of Excellence, you must begin to prepare for your journey by establishing core values. A core value is a personal belief reinforced by how you spend your time and treat other people. These core values will provide an internal guide to direct you on your journey and will reflect how you approach your pursuit of excellence and how you lead. These values will provide your safety net for when you fall. And make no mistake – when you hike the mountains that we will, you will fall. *Falls are to be embraced and encouraged, not avoided. Each fall serves as a learning experience, failure is positive feedback.*

CAIN'S COACHING POINT:
Reflect upon the following question: How do you want to be remembered when your last journey is over? What do you want people to say about you at the celebration of your life as an athletic administrator who was committed to the pursuit of excellence? As you think about this, write down the core values you will strive to embody over the course of this season and how you want to be remembered. Answering the question of how you want to be remembered when your life's journey is complete will help provide clarity to what is most significant to you and how you will want to begin living your life today.

_____

_____

As you reflect upon this big question, consider how your core values transfer to your AD performance. Think about how you would like people to acknowledge you and your contributions to your programs, school, and community over the coming season.

DIFFERENT VALUES FOR DIFFERENT TIMES

The reason we transition focus to a set of core values for the present season and not for an entire lifetime is that a lifetime is a daunting time frame. A lifetime is too difficult to imagine and therefore presents an intimidating mountain to climb.

It's important to focus on how you want to live over the course of the season in order to focus on how you must live in the present moment. Establishing this perspective will make climbing your mountain appear much more manageable.

Once you have identified what you want people to say about you and have reflected this in your core values, start living them "Today." These core values are fundamental principles that should be integrated into the routines of your daily life. If you are not regularly practicing these values, you will end up losing your way to the summit.

CAIN'S COACHING POINT:
The secrets of success are hidden in the routines of our daily lives. You will be as successful as your routines allow you to be on a daily basis. Start establishing routines and habits of excellence.

APPLYING CORE VALUES TO LIFE

When you look to the future, you may think it's difficult to have a commitment to excellence, have confidence and self-discipline for your entire life. This may be true, but you CAN live with a commitment to excellence, confidence and self-discipline "Today." With this perspective, you have an appropriately sized mountain to climb "Today." And then, do it all over again when tomorrow becomes "Today."

To begin applying core values to athletic administration and your life, choose one or two and focus on them for a set period of time.

CAIN'S COACHING POINT:
I recommend working on your specific core values for 1-5 weeks. Research shows it takes 21-28 days for positive personal change to occur with a focused plan and accountability partner. Right now, look over your core values and ask yourself, "How do I apply my core values in my life at this present time?"

Imagine it is the month of January and one of your core values is being passionate. As you commit yourself to working on being passionate this month, think about the following:

How would I define passion?

_____

_____

What does passion look like in the different aspects of my life?

_____

_____

What does passion look like in school, at games, and in the community?

_____

_____

_____

To provide myself a point of reference and to give myself a chance at living with passion I want to specifically know what passion looks like in those areas?

Answering all of these questions is significant to defining exactly what it is and how you plan on living this core value. If you specifically outline your core values, you give yourself the best chance for success in living them.

By establishing what it looks like for you to live your core values, you set yourself up for success. *It is easier to act your way into thinking and feeling than it is to think and feel your way into action.*

Knowing what action you must take and how you will take it to become the new-and-improved version of yourself sets the stage for a successful journey up the mountain.

When establishing your core values, I suggest you focus on between one and three for a given period of time. Initially, setting more than three would be an overwhelming endeavor. Giving yourself a more narrowed focus will increase your chances for successful mastery of a particular core value. If you can focus on being passionate for the month of January, you are going to be passionate beyond January into February. You may work up to having three or five core values over time. As with most anything, start small, get some wins under your belt, and then go bigger.

SUCCESS LEAVES CLUES

Here is some insight into achieving a successful career in anything you do: *Success leaves clues.* If you want to be a millionaire, go hang out with people who are millionaires. If you hang out with people who are making $50,000 a year and you tell them you want to make a million dollars a year, what are they going to do? They are going to laugh at you, because they do not see it as a reality. If you go hang around people who make a million dollars a year, you will get some ideas on how to make your first million.

The same rationale is true for athletic administration. You always hear coaches telling players, "If you want to get better, play with people who are better than you." This is because when you play with better players, you begin to pick up the clues to their success.

Imitation and adaptation to higher levels of competition will ultimately lead to performance improvement and success of your own. For you to become better as an administrator you need to surround yourself with people who are at the top of the game and you will pick up habits and characteristics they display.

> "Associate yourself with men of good quality if you esteem your own reputation, for 'tis better to be alone than in bad company."
>
> **George Washington**
> **1st President of The United States of America**

SURROUND YOURSELF WITH BETTER STUDENTS

To further illustrate the importance of hanging out with the right crowd, I will share a personal story from high school. When I was a high school student, I was not great academically. I reached a point where I knew I needed to improve my grades to play college baseball. I made a self-improving adjustment in my life and began surrounding myself with those who were academically more successful. I started to study with my teammates who excelled in the classroom and in a short period of time I became a better student. Rather than go play video games or watch TV, I would go to their houses or the library at Williams College in the town I grew up in, and shifted my focus to being the best I could possibly be. Excellence is a lifestyle, not an event, and this became apparent in all areas of my life.

CAIN'S COACHING POINT:
If you want more in a certain area of your life, you must become more. You become more by associating with those who are more than you in that area. You will become the average of the five people you associate with most. Pick wisely.

I didn't feel like going to the library, but I went anyway. The best students had a pre-established discipline that I knew I needed to develop.

I began noticing their study habits, and I started to learn that there are techniques you can use that are very simple to help with memorization and knowledge acquisition. When I began to imitate them, I started to get better results.

Success is largely about discovering a winning formula and implementing the system that facilitates excellence. Mastering the mental game is no different. If you surround yourself with those devoted to performance excellence, your chances of achieving it will drastically improve. When you invest your time properly into a winning system in the pursuit of excellence, success will take care of itself.

> "Managing your time without setting priorities is like shooting randomly and calling whatever you hit the target."
>
> **Peter Turla**
> **Former NASA Rocket Designer**
> **President, The National Management Institute**

DAILY GOAL SETTING & TIME PRIORITIZATION

Beyond the establishment of core values, daily goal setting and time prioritization are important for establishing the routine discipline necessary for peak performance. *I used to call it time management, but have since learned that you will manage your time based on how you prioritize your time*; therefore, *time prioritization is one step before time management.*

CAIN'S COACHING POINT:
There is only ONE factor shared by every Athletic Director in the world. You all have only 86,400 seconds in a day. Most will spend time; you will INVEST time. If you are not efficient with your time, the competitors who are will pass you by. Learn to take control and advantage of your time, or your time will take control and advantage of you.

As an aspiring peak performer, you must find different ways to make the best investment of your time to accomplish the daily goals you set. Throughout this book, I will share with you techniques you can use to better invest your time. For example, a great technique for time prioritization is to take a dry erase marker and write on your bathroom mirror what you want to accomplish the next day. I once heard Marcus Luttrell, author of *The Lone Survivor,* talk about how he used this very technique.

I started doing this in college and have found it to be VERY effective. **When you look in your mirror, you are not seeing who you are. You are seeing who you are working to become.**

You are in your bathroom frequently throughout the day, and the writing on your mirror will remind you constantly of what you want to accomplish. It also provides an effective method of preparing for the next day. When you go to bed you will be relaxed, knowing you already have a jump-start on the next day. By simply preparing the night before, your daily goals will always be waiting for you on your mirror when you wake up.

CAIN'S COACHING POINT:
Champions prepare their day the night before. Be sure that you pack your bag; then lay out your clothes, breakfast and everything you need to start the next day with TOTAL DOMINATION before you go to bed.

THREE STEPS TO PERFORMANCE IMPROVEMENT

Whether it is practicing core values or prioritizing your time, peak performance is all about continuous personal development and necessary change. A key theme throughout this book is that if you want more, you must become more.

Championship-winning coaches and athletes know that they must first become champions of personal responsibility in daily excellence before winning championships. They also know this takes an understanding of how to make necessary adjustments to change their performance to attain successful results.

One of the most successful sport psychologists of all time was the late Harvey Dorfman, author of *The Mental Game of Baseball* and coach to some of the greatest athletes in the world. Having had the chance to ask Harvey the million-dollar question (What do you know now that you wish you knew then?), he taught me that there are three essential steps you must follow if you want to make a performance improvement:

1. Develop an *awareness* of what needs to change.

2. Develop a *strategy* for change.

3. *Implement the strategy* with an accountability partner and assess yourself regularly so that the necessary performance change can occur.

Most administrators fall short of significant performance improvement because they either lack the awareness of what they need to change, do not formulate an effective strategy for the change, fail to facilitate the strategy to bring about the necessary change, or have a "YES" partner rather than an accountability partner who tells them the truth. Without this three-step system of performance change, an athlete can never achieve the necessary performance improvement to achieve excellence.

INSTANT AWARENESS

Here's a prime example of the three steps of performance change:

I was working with an Athletic Director who was 20 pounds overweight. I had him wear a 20-pound backpack to help develop his awareness of what it felt like to be 20 pounds overweight, and also what it would feel like to lose the extra 20 pounds he was carrying.

He wore the backpack around campus all day, and at the end of the day came back to see me. He took off the pack and said he was exhausted. I made him put the pack back on and we went to a game. About halfway through I had him take it off, and after the game I asked how it felt moving around without the pack compared to how it felt with the pack on. He said it was like night and day.

I placed my hands on his shoulders, looked him in the eyes, and said, "When you shed that 20 pounds you told me you want to lose, you are going to feel this good every day. Think about how much better you are going to be for those that you lead." The light bulb turned on. He got it. It was a great way to get him to have INSTANT AWARENESS.

This AD went through an experience that immediately conveyed an awareness he would not have had otherwise. This experience demonstrated that, "When I lose the weight, I am going to feel like I do, right now, without that pack on." There is the awareness. Then we came up with a strategy for him to lose the weight that involved working with a sports nutrition coach named Jason Spector (@SpectorJason) who got him locked in on his macro nutrition numbers. He thus had a plan to follow and guess what... plans work when implemented!

Notice that this AD did two things: he made his goal public and he implemented the established strategies with multiple accountability partners to assure success. Only you can make the necessary improvements; nobody else can make your performance change. It is absolutely essential that you hold yourself accountable to your goals, and the best method is making your goals public. As one of his accountability partners, I talked to him once a week about his goal. After a number of months, he had dropped the 20 pounds, had more energy, more confidence and was performing better. He was also stronger physically and mentally, and realized that with the right strategy and system he could accomplish anything. **SO CAN YOU!**

As exhibited through this example, the change begins with an awareness of what needs to change. Once this is accomplished, a strategy must be developed for the change to occur. Finally, the accomplishment of positive change for performance improvement begins to manifest through the implementation of the developed strategy and consistent assessment with your accountability partners.   The three-step process to accomplishing anything, combined with the three steps of performance improvement, provides you with the fundamental mental conditioning tools to effectively and successfully utilize the material within this program.

SELF-ASSESSMENT: STOP – START – CONTINUE

In order to further initiate your personal development and facilitate the accomplishment of your goals, you must assess yourself to build self-awareness.   As an aspiring peak performer, you must assess your most recent performances to establish self-awareness of what you must improve in your pursuit of excellence.   Take a look at your last three days.   What are two actions or behaviors that you are doing that you need to STOP in order to achieve the goals that you have set?

CAIN'S COACHING POINT:
What I must STOP doing in order to achieve my goals:

1)_____

2)_____

Now I want you to write down what it is you must START doing to help you achieve your goals.

CAIN'S COACHING POINT:
What I must START doing in order to achieve my goals:

1)_____

2)_____

Now I want you to write down what it is you must CONTINUE doing to help you achieve your goals.

CAIN'S COACHING POINT:
What I must CONTINUE doing in order to achieve my goals:

1)_____

2)_____

The Stop, Start, and Continue activity is a very simple process that ought to be frequently practiced to provide self-assessment and to keep you moving up your mountain. It is a simple activity to keep yourself honest about your work effort, but it is often not performed enough.

SIMPLE vs. EASY

It is here that I will take a moment to address an important distinction in both mental conditioning and performance in general. For any performer, it is important to be aware of a very significant distinction between the words "simple" and "easy." Simple and easy are not synonymous. Just because something is simple in concept does not mean it is going to be easy to do. If all simple things were easy, everyone would perform their best each time out and no upsets would ever occur. There would be no reason to play the game on the field – you could play it on paper.

There are a lot of average people walking around who have excellence buried inside of them but who are not trained or not willing to harness their hidden, untapped potential. As you read this book, you must consistently work to adopt and implement the simple practices and techniques that make a significant difference in performance.

THE NEXT 200 FEET

Imagine you were to drive from your cabin to the base camp for the hike to the top of the Mountain of Excellence – the tallest mountain in the world. If you were to leave your cabin at midnight, could you drive from your cabin to base camp? The answer is a definitive "Yes." It will be dark out, but you have the ability to drive the entire way up to base camp in complete darkness because of your headlights. Your headlights allow you to travel anywhere in the dark, because they illuminate the next 200 feet (**#Next200ft**) of the path. Therefore, by simply focusing on the next 200 feet, it's possible to drive anywhere you want in complete darkness.

When you are driving the next 200 feet, animals may run out in front of you, you may have poor weather and road conditions to deal with and you may get a flat tire. These events symbolize the adversity you are sure to face on your journey, and they are all outside of your control. All you can do is **embrace the adversity** and do what is necessary to reach your destination. Keep driving 200 feet at a time.

DESTINATION DISEASE

When metaphorically hiking up the mountain, the biggest obstacle we face is our obsession with the end result, the destination. This destination disease is representative of whatever end result you desire — the championship, the respect from the community, a blossoming relationship with your administrative team and board members, or the Hall of Fame. Remember that **the destination is the disease and the journey is the reward.**

Excessive focus and time devoted to looking at the destination beyond the next 200 feet is a common mistake. People set their goals too far out in front of them without understanding, creating and implementing a process to get there. By focusing on the outcome, people become stationary dreamers as opposed to advancing toward their goal, 200 feet at a time.

This is, quite simply, inaction versus action: the dichotomy between thinkers and doers. This is the condition of people counting down the days until that dream comes true as opposed to making the days count in a proactive and productive pursuit of that goal or dream. A dream without action will remain a dream, while a dream with action becomes a goal achieved.

As you proceed through each chapter of this book, remember to focus on the next 200 feet as opposed to the summit of your mountain. This will prevent you from being overwhelmed at times, and will make the ascent more manageable. **Keep the process over the outcome and the journey over the destination.**

> "The biggest reward for a person's hard work and effort is not what they get for it in the end, but who they become in the process."
>
> *Eric Davis*
> *Athletic Director*
> *Hanford High School*

REFUSE THE URGE TO BE AVERAGE

As you start to apply the strategies in this book to your professional work and to your life, you will receive some criticism, and some people may make fun of you for your commitment to self-improvement and performance excellence. Do not listen to the voices of negativity, for they are the voices of the masses – they are the voices of the average.

> "Be a yardstick of quality. Some people aren't used to an environment where excellence is expected."
>
> *Steve Jobs*
> *Co-founder of Apple*

Average people and average teams are the best of the worst and the worst of the best; this is a terrible place to live. Do not settle for average; strive for excellence and set your sights on the summit. Reach the pinnacle of success by climbing the Mountain of Excellence with a focused determination on your goals and with a dedication to personal responsibility in your daily excellence. **As famed inspirational speaker Zig Ziglar said, "There are no traffic jams on the extra mile."**

START YOUR JOURNEY WITH ONE STEP

The rest of this book is devoted to your 9-week journey into athletic administrative excellence. The material within these chapters will give you the mental game skills to establish your blueprint for excellence. View each chapter as the next 200 feet and conquer the mountain that is this book. It's a journey that will hopefully culminate with a conference/state championship or a vast culture improvement in your department. Regardless of when you start the journey, however, this program will provide you with the knowledge and skills to make the progress necessary to reach the summit of your mountain.

IF IT IS TO BE, IT IS UP TO ME

Remember, YOUR OWNERSHIP of this program is what will make the difference. You can't just read the book. You must OWN THE BOOK. You must put this book into action.

The most powerful two-letter-word sentence in the English language summarizes what this journey is all about: *If it is to be, it is up to me.* Your success in athletic administration and in life is determined by a lot of factors, and no factor is more important than the person reading this right now... YOU!

It has been said that *it is the start that stops most people.* Don't wait. Get started. RIGHT NOW!

Remember, if you take the four middle letters out of "doN'T WAit!" you get "***DO IT!***"

So don't wait, ***DO IT!*** Get started on your journey up the Mountain of Excellence, TODAY!

CHAPTER #1 REVIEW

- PRIDE = Personal Responsibility In Daily Excellence

- Excellence is being at your best when it means the most – every single day.

- The Mountain of Excellence represents the obstacle one must conquer to reach his outcome goal at the summit.

- The journey up the Mountain of Excellence is a self-transformative endeavor an individual must take to become a peak performer.

- One cannot live at the summit – you have to keep hiking or you will die.

- There is no end to the pursuit of excellence, there is no finish line.

- Peak performance is a constant journey pursuing excellence, and demanding personal responsibility is this daily pursuit.

- Choose your Mountain of Excellence you desire to climb and conquer.

- Remember, you are allowed to climb more than one mountain, but should focus on one summit at a time.

- The Three Steps to Accomplishing Anything:
  1. Make a commitment to a goal.
  2. Make it public with an accountability partner.
  3. Work with a relentlessly positive energy today.

- Today is where we are, every day.

- A core value is a personal belief reinforced through a set of actions and behaviors on a daily basis.

- Live your core values and demonstrate what it looks like to live them in your key areas.

- It is easier to act your way into thinking and feeling than it is to think and feel your way into action.

- Success leaves clues.

- Surround yourself with those who are better than you.

- You become the average of the five people you associate with most.

- Take advantage of your time or time is going to take advantage of you.

- The Three Steps of Performance Change:
  1. Awareness
  2. Strategy
  3. Implementation of the strategy

- Frequent self-assessment is essential to establish performance awareness.

- Simple and easy are not synonymous.

- Focus on the next 200 feet of the task at hand.

- A dream without action will remain a dream, while a dream that motivates action has the opportunity to become a reality.

- Do not settle for average – it is the best of the worst and worst of the best.

- It is the start that stops most people, so get started TODAY!

CHAPTER #2

TODAY IS THE MOST IMPORTANT DAY OF YOUR LIFE

> "The two most important days in your life are the day you are born and the day you find out why."
>
> **Mark Twain**
> **Author**

VALUE THIS DAY

The number one complaint of all Athletic Administrators is how there is not enough time in the day. (That and parents, but for right now we're going to focus in on something we can control.) The task list continues to grow and the time slips away. The duties and responsibilities attached to this job are never-ending. We have all experienced how the day can get away from us rather quickly with more on our "To-Do List" than when the day started. The frustration mount, negative energy takes over and our impact weakens.

One of the biggest challenges in life, and in becoming a master of your mental game, is developing an appreciation for the value of the present moment and then effectively possessing the ability to channel your focus into this present moment and this day.

As a leader of your school, your community, and your home, you must first be a leader of yourself and TAKE OWNERSHIP for the life that you are living!

This mission focuses on the present. In this chapter you will develop an appreciation for the importance of the present, and you will learn how to develop your present-moment focus so you can compete one day at a time.

In the introduction, you learned about the mindset of peak performers. You started to identify your values and put your focus on the plan as to how you will summit your mountain. You learned the importance of concentrating on the next 200 feet and the disciplined commitment to the process necessary to climb to the summit. As a committed administrator and someone who wants to develop their mental toughness, you must understand that **you do not count the days – you make the days count.**

How do we actually make the days count? The first step is possession of a present-moment focus.

THE 30-SECOND DRILL

Before discussing the present, I want you to experience it. In the following exercise, I want you to live in the present moment by immersing yourself in a present-moment focus. This exercise was taught to me by my mentor, Dr. Ken Ravizza, and it is called the 30-Second Drill.

Now as you read this, I want you to invest 30 seconds of your time as if your life depended on what you were reading. Sit up straight in your chair with your feet flat on the floor and LOCK IN! Now, I want you to look at each word and hear it as if I am there inside your head speaking to you.

I want you to read every word with a commitment that if you could repeat what you just read, you would win a million dollars. Think of it as the Million Dollar Mentality, because when you engage and focus with this type of intent all the time, it will not be long before someone wants to pay you a million dollars to work with them.

Ready?

GET SET!

GO!

Give me 30 seconds.

For a short period of time you can do anything you want with your levels of attention, energy, and focus. Right now, the focus you are reading with is different than it was 10 seconds ago – feel that. You see, you are more locked in right now than you were 15 seconds ago – recognize that. You are currently demonstrating your ability to be into the present moment.

If you can focus like this without someone having to ask you, you are experiencing the result of present-moment mental toughness. So, while you read this chapter today, I want you to come back to this level of focus as many times as you can and lock in for 30 seconds at a time.

That is 30 seconds.

You can now space out for a moment.

Whew... I hope you felt the intensity of those 30 seconds.

If I asked you for 10 minutes of total undivided attention with that level of focus, you'd probably say, "Cain, that is crazy. There is no way I can read with that intensity for 10 minutes." I would agree.

It is the same way in life. You don't lock in for 10 emails or an hour-long administrative meeting; you lock in for one email and then do it again and again until you clean your inbox.

Challenge yourself to become a samurai warrior of the mental game, someone who is totally immersed in the present; and when you get distracted or space out, recognize that you are distracted. Then release and refocus back into the present.

FEEL THE PULSE OF THE DAY

When you think of the present-moment focus, compare it to watching a sports performance. For example, if you ever attend a game in a large baseball stadium and you go to the top row to watch, you will notice that there is a pulse to the game. As the pitcher goes into his windup, everybody steps into the present. The pitch is thrown. Everybody steps out.

There is a pulse to the game. There is a routine ebb and flow to the game where the players, and even the audience, enter the present, and exit that moment after the pitch occurs. It is a short, intense focus followed by a space-out. That process repeats itself over and over for about 300 pitches each game. Essentially, it is a much shorter version of the 30-second drill you experienced above.

As you read this chapter, you will develop an enhanced understanding of how to get yourself and others into the present moment. It's important to remember that you can get here, the present moment, anytime you want. It is all a matter of awareness and choice. **Be where your feet are.**

> "We shall never have more time. We have, and have always had, all the time there is. No object is served in waiting until next week or even until tomorrow. Keep going day in and day out. Concentrate on something useful. Having decided to achieve the task, achieve it at all costs."
>
> *Arnold Bennett*
> *English Author*

KNOW YOUR 86,400 & 168?

Imagine when you wake up tomorrow morning you have $86,400 in your bank account. This is money that you must spend that day. It cannot be transferred, saved, or invested. At the end of the day, all of the money that is left in your account is wiped clean. What would you do with that money if that was the scenario? Exactly. You would spend it and not get cheated of all of the awesome things you would do with it. Well, most people do not have that luxury in their bank accounts each day, financially speaking, but we do have that form of currency every single day in the form of time.

Time is one factor that you and the competition have in common. Every person on the planet starts with the same exact unit of measurement in which to smash the goals they have set. We have 86,400 seconds in our day and 168 hours in our week, whether we are happy, sad, fired up, or lazy. Too often, Athletic Administrators get bogged down by their day and the responsibilities that are met with on the job. I had one AD say to me that he wears about 10 different hats. I agreed with him, but then asked him this question: "Would you ever walk around with 10 hats on your head?" He quickly responded, "No. I would look ridiculous." I agreed and made my point, "How about you determine which hat you CHOOSE to wear, and only wear that hat until it's time to switch." The blank stare on his face was one of amazement how that had never occurred. Since that day, he has been more intentional with how he switches gears and roles in order to increase his efficiency by using the following technique.

STOP SPENDING TIME AND START INVESTING TIME

I want to help you begin to dominate your days and to maximize your potential as a leader. In order to effectively do so, we will need to plan your time much as a financial planner plans money. Here's the rationale. Time is life. You either spend it or invest it, and you want to be an investor, not a spender.

Let's practice by reading the next paragraph with greater intensity than you have any other in this book. Let's start by making the commitment to 30 seconds of pure focus. Please put your feet down flat on the ground, have a straight spine for an alert mind, and GO!

A lot of AD's came from a teaching and coaching background before they entered the field of athletic administration. Many continue in those roles when they become an AD. In the coaching world, if you're well prepared, you plan out every phase of practice down to the minute in order to get the most out of the time you have. The same thing is done in the classroom. However, people fail to do this in their own lives, and leave lots to chance or to how they feel. If you would be prepared on what drill is coming up next in basketball practice, why wouldn't you want to be prepared with how your time is being invested while at home? **It's about choices, and whether you want to take control of your day or let your day control you.** Whether you spend time or invest time.

Ok, that's 30 seconds. Space out.

Relax. Did you feel the difference? Did you feel more engaged and focused as you read that paragraph?

Today is the most important day of your life and the only one that you are living. Tomorrow has never been promised to us and never will be. All we have are the 86,400 seconds in this day to attack this life that you've been blessed with. The freedom that comes from TODAY helps to break the chains of all that is to be worried about in the future. Today is the tomorrow you worried about yesterday. If we continually cycle and allow our minds to be penetrated by negativity and doubt, we never maximize the precious moments that are with us right now.

One of my favorite poets is Edgar Guest. His piece titled "Tomorrow" helps to outline the mistake people make in not taking advantage of today.

> He was going to be all that a mortal should be,
> Tomorrow.
> No one should be kinder or braver than he,
> Tomorrow.
> A friend who was troubled and weary he knew,
> Who'd be glad of a lift and who needed it, too;
> On him he would call and see what he could do,
> Tomorrow.
> Each morning he stacked up the letters he'd write,
> Tomorrow.
> And thought of the folks he would fill with delight,
> Tomorrow.
> It was too bad, indeed, he was busy today,
> And hadn't a minute to stop on his way;
> More time he would have to give others, he'd say,
> Tomorrow.
> The greatest of workers this man would have been,
> Tomorrow.
> The world would have known him, had he ever seen
> Tomorrow.
> But the fact is he died and he faded from view,
> And all that he left here when living was through
> Was a mountain of things he intended to do,
> Tomorrow.

What incredible perspective on the importance of today and how we have this gift of life to leave a legacy that the world will know by serving others.

THE BLUEPRINT

You are going to practice this same technique, but starting simple and planning each hour. If you're reading this in the morning, write in what you plan to accomplish today. If you're reading this at night, write in what you plan to accomplish tomorrow.

4:00 am _____

5:00 am _____

6:00 am _____

7:00 am _____

8:00 am _____

9:00 am _____

10:00 am _____

11:00 am _____

12:00 pm _____

1:00 pm _____

2:00 pm _____

3:00 pm _____

4:00 pm _____

5:00 pm _____

6:00 pm _____

7:00 pm _____

8:00 pm _____

9:00 pm _____

10:00 pm _____

11:00 pm _____

12:00 pm _____

Tim Corbin, the head baseball coach at Vanderbilt University and a master of the mental game, is one of the most detail-orientated coaches I've ever met. He is always on top of his day and the wise investment that time is for him as a National Championship coach running one of the top programs in the country.

I have found that leaders who do follow a time investment plan have reduced stress levels, never complain about a lack of time, and are committed to their day by being intentional with their time. As an Athletic Administrator, your time is valuable while you are in the building, but even more so when outside of the building with your family. Choose wisely and enjoy grabbing hold of your day and owning it!

HOCUS-POCUS or FOCUS-REFOCUS

Realize that success in any endeavor is not the product of hocus-pocus magic. You are not going to be successful today because the moon and the sun and the stars and the galaxy just happen to line up for you. *You are going to be successful to the degree that you are able to focus, and then refocus when you become distracted.*

Success is not hocus-pocus magic; it is actually much simpler than that. Success is largely dictated by your ability to maintain present-moment focus on the tasks at hand. The key to developing an intense and productive focus is to recognize when you become distracted, take a deep breath, and then refocus your attention.

You will get distracted, because everyone does. The attainment of peak performance is contingent on the development of distraction awareness. *You must develop the ability to recognize when you are distracted and then refocus back into the moment.*

An easy way to remember this is to think, *If I want to WIN, I must focus on What's Important Now.* Focus on what you are doing right here in this moment and on accomplishing the tasks in the present moment.

WATCH OUT FOR FISH HOOKS

Through recognizing that we all get distracted from time to time, it is equally important to recognize what distracts us from our goal. The term "fish hooks" is symbolic of the negative thoughts from external stimuli that your mind can get caught on during your pursuit of excellence.

Fish hooks represent distractions beyond your control that you focus on, which deplete your energy and rip you away from performing your best and competing in the present. Examples of fish hooks could be obnoxious fans, parents, unprofessional coaches, emails, voicemails, etc. – all of which are outside of your control.

Ultimately, fish hooks are a hassle and a needless waste of your time. You must develop an awareness of them so you do not get hooked, and so that when you do, you can get off the gaff (what they call the barb on the fish hook in the angler's world) before getting ripped out of the water.

To further illustrate the application of fish hooks in performance, think of yourself as a fish. As a fish, you are swimming in a school up Administration River to the destination of Lake Excellence.

As you swim upstream, you need sustenance for your journey, so you dine on whatever you can find. You discover worms are an especially delicious but a rare treat. You have observed some of your teammates trying to eat worms dangling in the water, only to get stuck in the mouth with a fish hook.

You learn to be wary of fish hooks when you see a worm. If you accurately identify worms with fish hooks, you can actually still have a meal by eating around the hook. ***Thus, if you keep the presence of mind to inspect your worms carefully, you will give yourself the best chance to reach Lake Excellence, aka being the best version of yourself.***

In this analogy, the worms are the opportunities to learn and succeed on your journey to performance excellence, and the fish hooks are the external stimuli within those opportunities that could keep you from your forward progress. As a performer (or fish), you must stay in the present moment and strategically seize the opportunities for self-improvement.

You must focus on what you can control – your presence of mind – and work around the fish hooks that have the potential to hold you back. If you see the worm, don't forget to check for a fish hook.

Don't get hooked.

CAIN'S COACHING POINT:

I want you to identify three fish hooks that you deal with in your program. What distractions have a tendency to steal your focus and get you hooked away from the present and ...?

FISH HOOK #1 _____

FISH HOOK #2 _____

FISH HOOK #3 _____

CHANGE TAKES TIME

There is no magic cure in order for you to begin changing the structure of your days and being more purpose-driven in planning.

There are four stages of buy-in that each person encounters when new concepts are introduced:

1. It's not for me.
2. It's for others.
3. I will try it.
4. How did I do this any other way?

As you move through the four stages, keep in mind that this is about self-improvement and doing what is best for YOU; that will in turn be what's best for the others in your life. When you identify what you want to have happen, you will begin to take the necessary steps to make that happen. You are in control of your life and can be an active participant in that life, not a human on a treadmill just going through the motions. **Your time, and your life, are worth fighting for.**

> "Yesterday is history, tomorrow is a mystery, and today is a gift – that is why we call it the present."
>
> *Unknown*

CHAPTER #2 REVIEW

- Yesterday is history, tomorrow is a mystery, and today is a gift — that is why we call it the present.

- Do not count the days; make the days count.

- The present moment is a matter of awareness and choice.

- Success in athletic administration is not hocus-pocus. It's all about your ability to focus and refocus.

- Focus on WIN (What's Important Now).

- Beware of fish hooks and things you can't control.

- The time is now and the place is here.

CHAPTER #3

PROCESS, ROUTINES AND HABITS OF EXCELLENCE

"To be consistent over time you must be able to describe what you do as a process."

Jim Collins
Author of Good to Great

The ability to perform at a level of excellence on a consistent basis is the goal of all peak performers. As the previous chapter discussed, the maintenance of a present-moment focus will assist you in this goal; however, you must have something to focus on in the present moment during daily performance. *This "something" is the process.*

A peak performer's focus must always be on the process. By keeping focus on the present elements of the performance process, people give themselves the best opportunity to perform on the level of excellence. An excellent process will give the best chance for success in yielding excellent results, and performing a step-by-step process directed at excellence will get you up the mountain as quickly as possible.

Remember, the commitment and concentration on the next 200 feet will get you safely to your destination. Focus on being excellent on your journey step by step up the Mountain of Excellence, and you will be sure to reach the summit.

UNLEARN WHAT YOU HAVE LEARNED

The current athletic culture we live in is a bottom-line results-driven monster. The public will measure your success as an Athletic Administrator by the games your teams win. The kicker is that to win games you must not focus on winning, but on the process of winning. Coaches and athletes I work with often have to unlearn what they have learned to focus on in their sport – mainly, winning and focusing on other outcomes that are outside of their control vs.

processes that are within their control that give them the best chance for success.

A peak performer must understand that winning is the outcome of performance excellence – thus, the by-product of an individual's or team's performance. The focus of the individual athlete and team, therefore, ought to be their performance, because that is what is truly within their control and yields the desired outcome. More precisely, a performer's focus should be on the process of his performance and directly on what he can control to provide the best opportunity for success.

CAIN'S COACHING POINT:
You must often unlearn what you have learned and realize that what got you here might not get you there. You must always be asking yourself, Why are we doing it this way? Is this the best way?

DAILY PROCESSES FOR FUTURE SUCCESSES

As an Athletic Administrator whose time is already stretched, we learned in the previous chapter about the importance of TODAY. Taking into account that you are a sum of your todays, there are items inside each day, think of them as quarters or possessions, that you must maximize in order to get the most out of that moment before the next one arrives.

There are 3 areas in an Athletic Administrator's life that require a process, so you do not get sucked into a black hole and lost without any chance of rescue. These three items are: email, phone calls/voicemails, and meetings. If you can utilize each of these processes, you will find that it does not cost as much time as it once did, and that you have now begun to function at a level that will allow you to *focus on productivity not activity.*

INBOX ZERO EMAIL MANAGEMENT SYSTEM

In any TV show that focuses on the transformation of one's body and weight loss, there is a standard procedure that each fitness trainer takes their client through – the cleaning of the cupboards from all of the junk. That is what we are going to do here, eliminate the items in your inbox that no longer have any bearing on what you do today and bog you down from professional progress.

Step 1: Look at the number of emails in your inbox and write that number down here _____.

Congratulations, you will no longer have this many emails screaming at you and sucking away your precious energy. I have seen numbers in the twenties to numbers in the thousands. They key here is to sift through what is needed and what is not.

Step 2: Create 3 separate folders in your Inbox and title them:
1. Reply + 2 minutes
2. Waiting for Action
3. Archived

Each folder has a very specific purpose intended for you to file the emails that enter your Inbox. To begin, there is a big difference between checking your email and processing your email. Checking email is time-consuming, exhausting, and takes you away from the task at hand (fish hook). Processing email is specific about the timing, invigorating, and allows you to lock in on the task at hand.

Step 3: Process your entire Inbox and move them to the folders based upon the description. At the end of your Inbox cleaning, you should have zero emails in your Inbox.

1. Reply + 2 minutes: Two minutes is the magical time frame at hand that will decide if an email goes here. These are emails that you need to reply to but will take longer than 2 minutes. Also included are the emails that will take you longer than 2 minutes to read and determine a response.

2. Waiting for Action: These emails that are awaiting a response or for somebody to do something for you. As an Athletic

Administrator, this could be used for uniform quotes, informational letters surrounding an upcoming tournament/event, or a conversation that is happening with another administrator.

3. Archived: This folder is for emails that do not fit into the above two categories, that you're holding onto for documentation but will never revisit unless needed. Most AD's will create folders in their Inbox and use this as an archives area; we encourage you to put those folders into your archives folder so that you have three main folders.

Now that your Inbox is at zero, the process surrounding email will become different than what you have done in the past. Remember, we are creating a new version of you, a better version of you, one that is taking full advantage of your time. When you plan your day, you will plan the time to process email and then to reply to your +2 minute folder.

This can be 3-4 times a day, at a time you can fully dedicate your effort into managing your Inbox, with the goal of getting your Inbox to zero at least once every 24 hours.

With any new email, the goal is to touch the email once and then execute the 4D System:

1. Delete it.
2. Delegate.
3. Do it (as long as it's under 2 minutes).
4. Drag it to the Reply + 2 minutes folder.

Now you begin to answer emails on your time, when it is convenient to you, and break the chains to your email. By setting aside 15 minutes to process email, you can handle all of your replies in time, so that you do not operate in a disorganized fashion and eliminate the items you no longer need.

PHONE CALL/VOICEMAIL ABSOLUTES

The blinking red light on your office phone or the voicemail message on your phone can cause alarm or distress. It all depends on how you view it. Most will think, "Oh great. What now?" Having a process for your phone calls will allow you to keep a 3-minute conversation from expanding into 30 minutes and eating away precious moments that you have set in your agenda. This must be scheduled time in your day with a frequency of 2-3 times, depending upon the situation. Keep in mind that you still need to operate at a professional level and respect the time of others. Most phone calls can be returned that day out of courtesy to the caller, and many of them can be replied to via email.

When a voicemail is received, be certain to document what you are hearing: who the caller is, when they called, what is a number to reach them, and what they want. Gathering those simple facts into a logbook will help you to keep documentation of the contacts you make via the phone. This can be done electronically or in a notebook.

When returning the call, a clear introduction is needed, giving first and last names and what institution you represent. Regardless if you know the person, that repetition in all calls will become second nature and will be a part of all business calls made. The most important part of this section is to **keep the conversation moving forward.** Do not be sucked in by small talk and stops in the action. Address what it is the person wants, and after the conversation has been finished, there's no need to continue.

Each of you has your repeat offenders and those who call frequently. You know the time that it will take to satisfy them, and sometimes that is 30 minutes. However, being a leader means listening to others and being available to discuss matters. This should not come at a time when your family, staff, or students are going to be placed on the back burner. Pick your time slot wisely in which to fit it. Sometimes it cannot be helped, but more often than not you will take control of when these happen. Get in, get it done and get out. With email, phone calls and now, meetings.

MEETINGS

Every Athletic Administrator has meetings to attend at the conference, district, state, and national level in order to conduct their business. These meetings are vital, for Athletic Administrators are completely dependent upon one another. Conferences must be on the same page in a broad variety of areas, such as officials' pay, scheduling, and by-laws. The meetings held within these categories are very well organized and allow you to block off your time fairly easily for travel and time on task.

The problem meetings are the ones that happen within your own building. These are the drop-by encounters that can drain away precious moments that you have planned to use to tackle your agenda items.

The same principles can be applied to these meetings as to email and phone calls/voicemails – it's all about the process.

As you plan each day, be sure to implement a time frame for each of the following:
1. Morning greetings
2. Establish office hours
3. Evening sendoff

Morning greetings consist of your taking 10-30 minutes before classes start and hit up the coaches, teachers, support staff, and secretaries with positive energy that will help set the tone for their day. This depends upon the structure of your school, the size and the campus, so tailor-make the time frame for what works for you.

Most of the people you encounter will have little to say or add, but those who need your help on an issue or question can get it within the 1-3 minutes around that person. Instead of the coach or staff members bringing themselves to you in your office, you are bringing yourself to them.

Establishing office hours has to do with your fighting for your time. You can post these on your office door or send out a document outlining what your schedule is throughout the day, and when you are free for people to visit. Each teacher and coach has a different schedule as well, so this will allow for appropriate planning and communication within the department. If a time cannot be arranged, you can pencil that person in for a larger chunk of time in your morning greetings or evening sendoff.

The evening sendoff is similar to the morning greetings. You are making yourself visible and available to others in small chunks. As a leader of the athletic department and of the entire school district, people want and need to see you. This pertains to the administration, student body, and staff. By being visible, you are making a conscious choice to get out of your office and on your feet to help give the people what they want.

> "We are what we repeatedly do. Excellence, therefore, is not an act but a habit."
>
> **Aristotle**
> **Greek Philosopher & Scientist**

THE IMPORTANCE OF ROUTINES

Having present-moment focus and being process-oriented not only gives you the best chance for success today, but is also the best predictor of future success. The best indicator of future behavior is past behavior. By establishing clear and consistent routines for your daily life, you will be fully immersed in becoming a person of action and a master of the mental game.

Routines are what you do each and every day with intention. It is a mindset that is bigger than your "To Do" list. This is more about creating your "To Dominate" list.

THE ATHLETIC DIRECTOR'S DAILY LIST

When planning your day, there are items that you must schedule in order to be effective as a leader at your school, your home, and within yourself. Each day, or close to it, you need to schedule:
- Working out
- Sleep
- Eating and food preparation
- Rest & Recovery
- Getting ready (showering, clothes, brush teeth, laundry)
- Meetings
- Masters Homework/Classes
- Lesson Planning/Grading
- Social Time – friends/family/staff

- Free Time
- Faith Observation
- Spouse/Significant other

These items are going to help you to operate at a highly functional level so that you can best perform the duties of Athletic Administrator. Burnout happens when one forgets about their own self and they notice their health, relationships, and attitude deteriorate. Planning these items within your schedule every day will help to maintain strong physical, mental, and social health.

If you recall in the previous chapter, you planned out your day from when you rise to when you sleep. Every person has a morning routine that they follow which gets them started to dominate the day.

Write out your morning routine, from when you wake up to when you arrive at the office.

_____
_____
_____
_____

How many of the items from the Athletic Directors Daily List did you write down? Having a quality morning routine to get yourself ready will keep you on the path to present-moment focus and to being your best on a consistent basis.

Write out your routine from when you arrive at the office to your first class/meeting/commitment.

_____
_____
_____
_____

At this point in time, you have created a plan of attack for you to get the most out of your time and to have a process for what you do. ***Nothing happens by accident in the lives of those who are the most successful people on the planet.*** As you develop further, this will become a part of who you are, and will positively impact all facets of this life you are leading and living.

HABITS OF EXCELLENCE

I am your constant companion.
I am your greatest helper or your heaviest burden.
I will push you onward or drag you down to failure.
I am completely at your command.
Half the things you do, you might just as well turn over me,
and I will be able to do them quickly and correctly.
I am easily managed; you must merely be firm with me.
Show me exactly how you want something done,
and after a few lessons I will do it automatically.
I am the servant of all great men.
And alas, of all failures as well.
Those who are great, I have made great.
Those who are failures, I have made failures.
I am not a machine,
though I work with all the precision of a machine
plus, the intelligence of a man.
You may run me for profit, or run me for ruin;
it makes no difference to me.
Take me, train me, be firm with me
and I will put the world at your feet.
Be easy with me, and I will destroy you.
Who am I?
I am a HABIT!

This is one of my favorite poems. Habits are a distinct part of the process and what you do on a daily basis to ensure the success of the gift you have been given – the present and this day. Habits often have a negative connotation associated with them because they are interpreted as vices. These tend to drag one down, instead of building one up. The view we will take is to build you up and to solidify your mental game as you hike up the Mountain of Excellence.

Simply put, habits are what you do within your daily routines. There are many Habits of Excellence that I suggest to add to different routines in your day. The parts of the day that one has the most control over are the morning and evening routines. Here are a few habits I highly recommend:

Morning

1. Make your bed – this symbolic task triggers your mind that sleep time is over and domination time is here

2. Call Success Hotline – Dr. Rob Gilbert is a mentor of mine and a master of the mental game. He records a daily motivational message that you can call and listen to, to help create an elite mindset every day. (973) 743-4690.

3. Read *The Daily Dominator* – this book was inspired by *The Maxwell Daily Reader* by John Maxwell. The daily entries are short and map out 365 days of mental conditioning

Evening

1. Phone Timeout – make all calls on your drive home; upon entering your home, put your phone on vibrate/silent and place it in a designated spot for the rest of your night. This will help you be the husband/wife and father/mother you need to be.

2. Clothes set out – you will salvage precious minutes of your morning by selecting your clothes the night before and laying them out. No longer will you stare at your closet wondering what to wear.

3. Bag Check – go through your bag or briefcase to ensure that you have everything you need to start the next day. There is great peace of mind that comes from knowing you do not have to hesitate when walking out the door towards your mission.

Your habits will determine the success of your routines which will determine the success of your process. Having the correct mindset will lead to the outcome you want in your performance. **Habits + Mindset = Peak Performance.** Establishing successful habits is to do a little a lot, not a lot a little. It is the stop that starts most people, due to the fact that they try to create too many habits at once.

A locomotive spins its wheels for the first few revolutions when the engine kicks in. Trust in your process: the wheels will stick, you will build momentum, and you will become unstoppable.

CONTROL WHAT YOU CAN CONTROL

A huge part of the process is controlling what you can control and letting the outcome take care of itself. When the "best teams" show a mental lapse, the underdog is usually right there ready to seize the moment. We can, thus, definitively state that the "best team" never wins; it is always the team that plays the best.

The Athletic Administrators who best understand the significance of the process over the outcome have established proficiency for recognizing what they can control and what they cannot. It is amazing how many administrators still get hung up and hooked on things outside of their control. If you want to become a peak performer in this profession, you must learn how to differentiate between what you can control, what you can influence, and what you cannot control.

When you put time and energy into things you cannot control, you are wasting both of those valuable resources. Focusing on these things is self-defeating and assists the opposition in the process. Peak performers in athletics do not operate that way; they stay locked in on what they can control.

Here is a list of things you cannot control in your role as Athletic Administrator: you cannot control the referees, your fans, the opposing team's fans, the media, PARENTS (more on that later), the weather, what others think of you, the amount of hot dogs remaining in the concession stand, the views of other Athletic Administrators, the administration at your school, and the outcome of the event you're attending. **The only thing you can control is yourself and your APE.** APE is an acronym for your **A**ttitude and appearance (body language); your **P**ositive self-talk, presence (focus), process (preparation), performance (how hard you compete/work), perspective; and your **E**ffort, energy and emotions.

WHAT CAN YOU CONTROL?

CAIN'S COACHING POINT:

As mentioned above, a huge component of the process is controlling what you can control. In the space provided below, write down in the first column all of the things that you can control, and then list the things that you cannot control in the second column.

CAN CONTROL   **CANNOT CONTROL**

_____   _____

_____   _____

_____   _____

_____   _____

_____   _____

_____   _____

_____   _____

_____   _____

_____   _____

Look at the list of things you cannot control. If you choose to focus on these things, you will inevitably beat yourself. If you choose to focus on these things, you are getting hooked. You must keep your focus on what you can control. If you go to YouTube and watch the TCU Baseball _Quiet Confidence_ video, you will hear Coach Schlossnagle talking about how they focus on attitude and effort and everything else is a complete waste of time. If you have not viewed it yet, check it out now and learn from one of the best programs in the nation.

APE

As a peak performer, you must focus your attention on what is within your control. External adversity is a part of life – you make the choice of how you react to it. APE provides you with a reminder of just what it is you have the ability to control.

APE is an acronym to remember that you control:

A – Your attitude and your appearance (body language)

P – Your perspective (how you see things), the process (how you choose to play), your preparation, your presence (focus) and your self-talk (positive)

E – Your effort, your energy, and your emotions

This acronym is symbolic of the concept "control what you can control." This concept is a fundamental skill of mental conditioning. Self-control is essential to peak performance, and by the end of this book you will fully understand why you only have control over yourself in the midst of performance. As my mentor, Dr. Ken Ravizza, would say, *1. You have got to be in control of yourself before you can control your performance* and *2. You have very little control of what goes on around you but total control of how you choose to respond to it.*

MY GOAL MUST BE IN MY CONTROL

All athletes, coaches, and Athletic Administrators will agree that goal setting is a critical part of the process in climbing your Mountain of Excellence. When setting performance goals, you must remember that *your goal must be within your control. A common mistake made in goal setting is setting performance goals that focus on the desired outcome instead of setting goals that reflect the process that you must execute to get the desired outcome.*

THE BEST ADMINISTRATORS FOCUS ON THE PROCESS

The best Athletic Administrators know the value of focusing on the process. They see the process as a staircase they climb each day. They know what their desired outcome is and focus on that outcome 20% of the time, while focusing 80% of the time on TODAY and the steps they must take to get the outcome they desire.

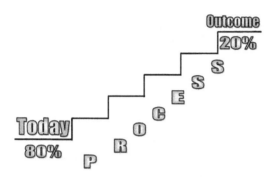

My challenge for you is to begin committing yourself to the process. Start evaluating your performance on the process it takes to perform at a level of excellence. Focus on the effort you give every day. Focus on executing the fundamentals when you perform in meetings and during event management. As an athletic department, focus on bringing great energy and intensity, supporting each other with excellent participation, and always demonstrating strong body language.

CAIN'S COACHING POINT:
What are some aspects of the process that, if you focused on them, would give you the best chance to perform at your best?

1) _____

2) _____

THERE ARE NO LITTLE THINGS

It's worth emphasizing explicitly that there are no little things in the pursuit of excellence in athletic administration. As alluded to in the previous section, one must also recognize and appreciate all the little details of peak performance within athletics to become a peak performer. When you are fully committed to the process of becoming a peak performer, you must be aware of all the details of your performance process, for they are necessary to make a successful journey to the summit of the Mountain of Excellence.

KEEP YOUR LOWS HIGH AND YOUR HIGHS LOW

Emotional consistency is essential for success in any profession, especially that of an Athletic Administrator. The goal of those striving for success in any arena is to maintain performance excellence day in and day out. The control of emotions is imperative for consistent peak performance.

When you are faced with adversity and your performance is not reflective of your potential, it is crucial to take a step back from your performance and focus on the process of excellence. *Command your emotions by reminding yourself to control what you can control; focus on releasing the mental bricks that can weigh on your mind by having a physical release that you can use, such as shutting the lid on your laptop and taking a deep breath.*

Resist the pressure to personalize performance and remember that being an Athletic Administrator is what you do, not who you are. If you have a bad day at the office, that does not make you a worthless human being, just as having a career day does not make you any better than anyone else once that day is over.

By paying attention to the process and not the outcome, you give yourself the best opportunity to achieve excellence, because if you focus on the process and make the necessary changes to it, the result will take care of itself.

The same systematic process is true when you are performing at your best. When you are performing at your highest level and achieving success through performance excellence, it is crucial that you not become complacent. Resist the urge to buy into the hype. Do not think that a little success suddenly renders you more valuable than the process that got you there. Cemeteries are full of irreplaceable men. Stay humble. Continue to work the process. Give yourself the best opportunity to maintain the excellence you have been achieving by identifying the process you followed to get there, and then keep refining that process by making it more efficient and excellent.

On the following page is a "sign of success" from the one of the top college athletic programs in the country. This image is testament to the program's understanding that you must focus on the process of becoming a champion in order to win championships.

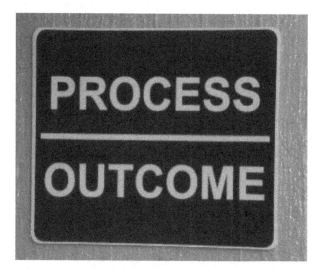

It is challenging to commit oneself to the process of performance excellence. The journey is long and hard, full of obstacles and detours, but this is what makes the glory of achieving performance excellence all the more glorious. *Remember, nothing worth having comes easily. Your enjoyment in the end will be a direct reflection of the effort you had to give in the process of becoming who you needed to become to be worthy of getting what you wanted.*

"The true worth of a man is to be measured by the objects he pursues."

Marcus Aurelius
Roman Emperor

DEVOTE YOURSELF TO THE PROCESS

Commitment to the process of excellent performance will give you the best opportunity to achieve your goals. In this chapter, you have learned that when you devote yourself to the process, you focus on the aspects of performance within your control as opposed to the elements beyond it. You now understand that maintaining control of the process of your pursuit of performance excellence is a means to getting your desired outcome and end result.

Unfortunately, it is common for most people in athletics to become fixated on the goal/outcome/end result of performance. As an aspiring peak performer, focus on what you need to do to achieve the outcome and the results you desire. Devoting yourself to the process of performance excellence will undoubtedly give you the best chance to win and, more importantly, to reach the summit of the Mountain of Excellence this season and in your life.

CHAPTER #3 REVIEW

- Unlearn what you have learned about winning.

- Process should always be placed before the outcome.

- Performance Excellence is greater than winning.

- The best team never wins. It is always the team that plays the best.

- Control what you can control.

- Develop self-control over your APE.

- Winning is a by-product of excellent execution of the fundamentals and focusing on the process over the outcome.

- There are no little things.

- Keep your lows high and your highs low – emotional consistency is essential for peak performance.

- Make "signs of success."

- Nothing worth having comes easily.

- When you devote yourself to an excellent process, the result will take care of itself.

CHAPTER #4

THE VALUE IN A
POSITIVE MENTALITY

"Be responsible for the positive energy that you bring."

Mike O'Day
NIAAA Hall of Fame Athletic Director

Negativity is all around us. Turn on the news each day, and it is plastered with all that is wrong in the world and the tragedies that take place. There is no surprise why people act the way they do – we have been conditioned to be pessimists. The role of Athletic Administrator is no different; the negativity that comes our way makes our schools and programs seemed doomed to failure. Every administrator is forced to deal with problematic issues and complaints every single day. As one is immersed into an environment, they will eventually become like that environment. *People are products of their environments.*

If we were to create a poll comparing the positives and negatives of the job of Athletic Administrator, the negative list would fill up much faster, due to the fact that negative situations jump out at us and we take positive moments for granted. The individual's mindset is the main variable that will allows one to focus on the positive or the negative.

The power of positive self-talk and a positive mindset makes a huge difference in an individual's performance. It is a simple concept that is both useful and effective. Having a positive mentality is so simple that it is often overlooked. It's so easy to do that it's easy not to do it.

We're used to hearing people tell us to "think positive" during times of adversity or general advice from one person to another, but the words often roll in one ear and out the other, without our full appreciation of the true value in this all-too-simple piece of advice. Having positive self-talk (the voice inside your head) with a positive mentality is a mental skill that requires proper mental conditioning to utilize its power. The magnificent quality of positivity is that everyone is capable of it. It is simply a mental attitude that is conducive to growth and excellence through the expectation and perception of favorable and beneficial results. This chapter is devoted to conveying the importance of positivity in your daily performance while presenting you with the strategies you need to develop your own positive mentality.

THE PROPHECY OF THOUGHT

The basic tenet is that whatever the mind expects, it will attract. This "law of attraction" has been proven with neuroscience. Thoughts manifest through actions and affect outcomes. If you are doubtful you will accomplish a task, you drastically increase the likelihood that your actions and effort will reflect that doubt, thus ensuring the failure of accomplishment. Similarly, if you possess a positive mentality when faced with a difficult task, you dramatically increase the likelihood that your actions and effort will reflect that positive attitude, and you will succeed.

THE SCIENCE OF STAYING POSITIVE

Research has proven that staying positive will make a big difference in your life.

Positive people live longer. In a study of nuns, those who regularly expressed positive emotions lived an average of 10 years longer than those who didn't (Snowdon, 2001).

Employees who perceive their work environments as positive vs. negative outperform their negative counterparts (Goleman, 2011).

Positive and optimistic salespeople sell more than pessimistic salespeople (Seligman, 2006).

Marriages are more likely to succeed when the couple experiences a 5-to-1 ratio of positive to negative interactions, whereas when the ratio approaches 1-to-1, marriages are more likely to end in divorce (Gottman, 1999).

Positive people who regularly express positive emotions are more resilient when facing stress, challenges and adversity. Athletic

Administration is full of stress, challenges and adversity.

Athletics also are full of negative events and negative people. Robert Cross, a researcher at the University of Virginia, found that 90% of anxiety at work is created by 5% of one's team or staff – those energy vampires that SUCK the life out of you. Make sure YOU ARE NOT a 5-percenter on your team or on your staff.

POSITIVE THINKING IS NOT ENOUGH

The successful accomplishment of a task, however, is not guaranteed by positive thoughts. All a positive mentality does is significantly increase the probability that you will walk away from the task, successfully accomplished or not, with greater experience and with greater peace of mind. In this way, a positive mentality makes a significant difference between educational self-improvement (growth) and self-stagnation (death). Thus, your mentality represents the ultimate self-fulfilling prophecy. Thoughts Become Things **(#TBT).**

THE STORY OF ROGER BANNISTER

 On May 6, 1954, Roger Bannister, a British medical student and avid runner, did the previously unimaginable. From the earliest archived world records and modern timekeeping in track events, no one had been able to break the seemingly impassable barrier of the 4-minute mile. His story demonstrates the prophecy of thought and the power of positive belief.

At the age of 25, the British sports media had already discovered Bannister, who had become one of the most scrutinized track athletes in the United Kingdom. His speed in the mile and 1500-meter events drew initial attention to his talent, but when he declined the 1948 Olympics in London to concentrate on his training and medical studies, he drew the criticism of British track enthusiasts. In 1951, Bannister won the British title in the mile, but his fourth-place finish in the 1500-meter race at the 1952 Olympics in Helsinki – the result of a last-minute schedule change that compromised Bannister's preparation routines – fueled further scrutiny for his unconventional training regimen.

After the media publicized his Olympic performance as a failure, Bannister resolved to redeem himself by breaking the seemingly unbreakable 4-minute mile barrier. He increased the intensity of his training, but not the duration, and saw steady improvements in his times, all while he continued to be a full-time medical student. In fact, the duration of his training was less than an hour per day, because he wanted to focus on his study of neurology. Bannister, however, was committed to his new goal and **loyal to the process** he felt would get him there. He was convinced that, as long as he continued to see gradual improvements in his times, he would maintain his own training regimen.

The opportunity Bannister had been training for arrived on May 6, 1954, in a meet between the British Amateur Athletic Association and Oxford University at the Iffley Road Track in Oxford, England. Running mates Chris Chataway and Chris Brasher exchanged setting the pace for Bannister's first three laps. Bannister unleashed his kick in the last lap, finishing it in less than a minute before he broke the tape and collapsed into the arms of the crowd at the finish line.

The announcer affirmed what the crowd of roughly 3000 spectators already knew. To thunderous applause, it was announced that Bannister ran 3:59.4 – the unbreakable record had been broken and Roger Bannister had made history! He had made the impossible possible.

DEFEATING LIMITING BELIEFS

The 4-minute mile story, however, is not simply about the historic moment of a broken world record. The story of Roger Bannister is about breaking mental barriers and defeating limiting beliefs. At the time, the world of track and field believed the 4-minute mile was an insurmountable human barrier, an impassable obstacle that could not be breached. The critics said it couldn't be done and that it was physically impossible to run a mile in under four minutes. It was thought that the heart would stop, the brain would explode, and the lungs would collapse.

As the world scoffed at what it saw as an amateur athlete's unachievable dream, Bannister hardened his resolve to the pursuit of excellence. What makes his feat even more remarkable was that he was dedicated to attain excellence not only on the track, but also in his academic ambitions of becoming a doctor. Bannister believed in himself and he believed in the process to which he had committed himself. As long as steady improvements accrued, he knew the outcome he desired would take care of itself – and that is exactly what happened.

THE IMPORTANCE OF ROGER BANNISTER

After Bannister had debunked the myth of the 4-minute mile, other runners around the world began breaking the 4-minute mile barrier. The week after his historic performance, Bannister and two other runners ran a sub-four-minute mile. Over the course of the following year, thirteen more runners broke the barrier. Within the next two years, exactly 134 runners ran a mile under 4 minutes, and today over 20,000 have been recorded. On July 7, 1999, Hicham El Guerrouj of Berkane, Morocco, ran the current world record in 3:43:13. In 1997 Daniel Roman of Kenya ran two miles for the first time ever in under 8 minutes, in a time of 7:58:61.

This is evidence that there are no physical barriers, only self-limiting barriers. We are the ones who put up these barriers within our own psyche because we choose the beliefs of those around us. You need to unlearn these limitations and realize that, once mental barriers are lifted, anything is possible. Peak performers and champions perceive the world differently, and as perspectives change, the realm of possibility expands. My goal for you is to have no mental barriers, to believe you are capable of anything you desire and work toward with the right strategies.

Bannister proved all the naysayers wrong with his positive mentality and self-belief, and now is the time for you to do the same.

SELF-IMAGE OF EXCELLENCE

The field of peak performance has substantiated the notion that, as a performer, you will never outperform your self-image. If you believe you are slow, you will perform slowly. If you believe you are fast, you will perform at a fast pace. Therefore, positive thought processes, combined with clear goals and right strategies for how to accomplish them, will give you the best opportunity for success. In this way, staying positive is symbolic of belief in yourself.

A self-image of excellence is absolutely necessary if you are to embark on the quest to conquer the Mountain of Excellence. You must believe in yourself and your ability to improve throughout the process you have established to achieve your goals. You must believe in your inner excellence and its transcendence to the performances you give on a day-to-day basis. Self-image is a powerful tool in peak performance, which is why it is so important for you keep it positive.

INTRODUCTION TO SELF-TALK

When you are performing at your best, and your day is running smoothly on all cylinders, what are you thinking? When you are at your best, what types of words are going through your head? What's that self-talk like?

_____

_____

In peak performance, the little voice talking inside of your head, sometimes becoming outwardly expressed thoughts directed at yourself, is referred to as self-talk. This little voice inside your head talks to you constantly. You may be reading this and thinking: "What is this 'voice' Cain is talking about? I do not talk to myself, only crazy people do that." That would be the voice to which I am referring.

CAIN'S COACHING POINT:
When referring to self-talk, I often use the analogy of your two mental assassins. You have a green assassin that helps your performance and a red assassin that crushes your performance. You must train your green assassin to win the battle between your ears with positive self-talk.
Everybody has self-talk. As an expression of thought, self-talk embodies your mentality towards your performance. We

use self-talk to motivate ourselves and to calm ourselves down when stressed. We use self-talk to encourage ourselves to become fascinated and, unfortunately, self-talk can be used to discourage ourselves when we are frustrated. Self-talk is a reflection of self-image.

When you are performing in your daily tasks as administrator, the voice in your head is either working for you or against you. Some people visualize the contrasting tones of voice as two little people on your shoulders battling for control over your conscience. Recognize, however, that this self-talk is yours. You own it; you are in control of it.

> "Rule your mind or it will rule you."
>
> ***Horace***

HARNESS YOUR SELF-TALK

Mastering control of your self-talk can be a challenge. Imagine your self-talk is a mustang (not the car, the horse – and there is nothing better than driving a Mustang convertible with the top down and Metallica blasting on the radio!), a wild and spirited, seemingly uncontrollable mustang horse. Now, imagine yourself as a cowboy who does not wish to strip this wild animal of its fiery spirit, but you do want it to work for you to enhance your pursuit of excellence on the open plains – so you must gain control of the animal without taking away its aggressiveness. This is how to think of your self-talk. It is an untamed and powerful beast that has the potential to significantly improve your performance.

Many of the administrators, coaches, and athletes I work with describe their self-talk as an active voice but always under control. They often describe it as living and competing on the edge. ***One player said, "If I am not competing on the edge of my emotions and energy, highly engaged but on the controlled side of the line, I am taking up too much space."***
To effectively harness your self-talk, you must follow the three steps of performance improvement as earlier discussed. The first step in the process of channeling the power of your self-talk is to establish an awareness of its power over the mind. Try to recognize when

you use it and what mentality it reflects – positive or negative. Notice particular situations that bring it out, both the good and the bad. Notice the particular tones and language used. This is all in an attempt to understand your mental state during time on the job and also away from it.

Once you have developed a proficient awareness, the next step in effectively harnessing your self-talk is through a technique called confidence conditioning.

FOCUS ON WHAT YOU WANT VS. WANT TO AVOID THE PINK ELEPHANT

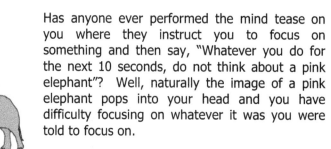

Has anyone ever performed the mind tease on you where they instruct you to focus on something and then say, "Whatever you do for the next 10 seconds, do not think about a pink elephant"? Well, naturally the image of a pink elephant pops into your head and you have difficulty focusing on whatever it was you were told to focus on.

This little mental tease exemplifies the importance of an individual's ability to keep a focus on what you "want" vs. "want to avoid," because the brain does not recognize the negative connotation of "do not" and only sees the image of that pink elephant.

The key to ignoring the pink elephant is to develop the ability to focus on what you are trying to accomplish, not on what you are trying to avoid. As an Athletic Administrator, if you are hosting an event, think about how well you can interact with those in attendance instead of guessing what will go wrong.

Academically, when you are taking a test, you want to focus on solving the problem or answering the question at hand, one question at a time, not worrying about the next question till you finish this one. These general scenarios represent the present-moment focus that makes the difference between subpar performance and performance excellence.

By channeling your self-talk and focusing on what you want vs. what you want to avoid, you will be competing with a positive mentality that will keep you locked into the present moment, giving yourself the best chance for success. The ability to focus on what you want with positive self-talk instead of on what you want to avoid is a discipline developed over time. This process is dependent on the establishment of routines, such as practicing your self-talk and strengthening your self-talk through the use of confidence-conditioning statements.

CONFIDENCE-CONDITIONING STATEMENTS

Confidence-conditioning statements are a mental conditioning technique used to harness the power of self-talk to work in your best interest. Confidence conditioning is accomplished by simply writing down a list of statements that give you a sense of strength and empowerment when you read them. You can put these confidence-conditioning statements on notebook covers, on the wall, on your mirror with a dry erase marker, in your locker, on little cards to carry in your wallet, as the background on your iPhone – or have them pop up as reminders on your iPhone (personally, this is how I do it). You can put them anywhere and everywhere.

Even though you may not be aware of it, you have been using confidence-conditioning statements ever since you could talk. Every time you expressed your belief in the truth of an idea or an experience, you were conditioning it. Mental imagery, which is simply the creation of vivid mental images, is a natural process as well. Whenever you imagined something or looked forward to it, you were using imagery and conditioning your subconscious mind. Confidence conditioning and mental imagery are used by a wide variety of people from virtually every walk of life and in every profession. They use these techniques because they are simple to learn, even easier to perform, and they work!

When written and/or put on audio, confidence-conditioning statements are your custom-made blueprint for personal growth and mindset achievement, providing a consistent state for your mental imagery and personal development. They are goal statements that help you imagine and realize positive change with minimal stress. If you use them correctly and consistently, they will help you create the athletic career, relationships and life you most desire.

In order to be effective, confidence-conditioning statements must be written and used in a way that has the desired impact on your subconscious mind. They must be brief, usually a short sentence, and phrased in the first person present tense. They must be positive, specific and realistic. You want to include as many details as possible when writing, and they should carry an emotional charge. If they do not make you feel anything, they probably will not help change anything either. *The test of whether a confidence-conditioning statement is written the right way is to ask yourself, "Can I read, picture and feel this statement?"*

CONFIDENCE CONDITIONING GUIDELINES

The following are guidelines to help you better write your confidence-conditioning statements:

First Person: Confidence-conditioning statements are tools that help you to change your self-image; therefore, it makes sense to mentally condition for yourself, because your statements are always about you. They will usually begin with "I."

Present Tense: Use the present tense (I am, I have, etc.) because, in your subconscious, the future and past do not exist. Subconscious time is always "right now."

Positive: Condition and image what you want, not what you do not want or are trying to change. Do not phrase a statement in the negative, such as, "I no longer get anxious when I address unruly parents." Instead say, "I remain calm, in control and focused on what I want to do in this conversation, for this is a part of my role as leader and I embrace it." This focuses on what you want to do in the present with a positive mentality.

Indicate Achievement, not ability or potential: In other words, do not say "I can." You already have the potential to change your performance. Instead, create words that describe the end result you want as if it has already happened by using "I am."

No Comparisons: You are unique and have your own process of personal development, growth and change.   Do not compare yourself to anyone else or measure your abilities against anyone else's. Just aim for and condition performance change in your own self-image and self-belief.

Vivid & Descriptive Language: In order to "convince" your subconscious that your confidence-conditioning statements are real, your language and the images they invoke must be as vivid as possible. Be sure to choose words that help you to really "see" what you are describing.

Emotional Language: Use words that spark an emotional response to make your statements more believable to your subconscious.   The more emotion you generate, the faster the change you seek will take place. Describe how you feel about your achievement.

Realistic/Accurate: Do not affirm change that isn't possible or realistic for you. Set your sights neither too high nor too low. Stretch your comfort zone a bit, but do not aim for anything you cannot honestly see yourself achieving.   Remember, peak performance is a process. Do not aim for perfection; aim for excellence.

Balance: Make sure that the various goals you condition are in balance with each other. Do not overemphasize any one area while ignoring others in which growth would be beneficial.   Strive for balanced growth and a balanced life.

Confidential: Without intending harm, others may remind you of your old self-image, or they may feel threatened by your desire to change. Keep your statements confidential. You may confide in mentors, if they understand the confidence-conditioning process and are supportive of the changes you are trying to make for the sake of your growth and performance.

TIPS FOR WRITING EFFECTIVE CONFIDENCE-CONDITIONING STATEMENTS

1. Change Your Beliefs Before Your Behavior:

It is pointless to condition new behavior when the underlying beliefs driving your old behavior remain unchanged. Write your confidence-conditioning statements for both internal beliefs and external behaviors. Failure to change underlying beliefs is one of the main reasons why confidence conditioning will not work for everyone.

BEHAVIOR: I spend an hour of quality one-on-one time with my significant other every night to strengthen our bond together.

BELIEF: More pressure on an already jammed-up schedule. I'd rather be mindless and watching TV without any distractions. When do I get my quality time away from it all?

Do you see the problem? If the underlying belief does not change, it will be impossible to sustain the new behavior. As long as it feels like something you "have to" do, and not something you "want to" do, your creative subconscious will find ways to get you out of it. Try this as an alternative:

BEHAVIOR: I enjoy spending an hour of quality one-on-one time with my significant other every night.

BELIEF: I look forward to spending time with my significant other every night because it's fun, leaves me feeling great about our relationship, and is building a stronger bond that will help us to perform better in this life we're living together.

2. Build Personal Value in Your Confidence-Conditioning Statements

The positive emotions you feel as you repeat and picture your statements is what makes them "take" in your subconscious. For example:

BELIEF: My health and fitness are major priorities in my life.

BEHAVIOR: I am creative at finding ways to exercise at least one hour a day, six days a week, and I generally eat only nutritious, macronutrient-rich foods.

PERSONAL VALUE: Because I exercise and eat right, I feel energized, strong, in control, and excellent.

3. Review Your Statements to Imprint Confidence into Your Subconscious

Imprinting is simple: READ or LISTEN to your confidence-conditioning statements, PICTURE them in your mind, and FEEL the personal value (positive emotions) connected to them. The best times to do this are just after awakening and just before sleep. Review your statements twice a day at a minimum, although more is often better. Make sure you are relaxed (take several deep breaths) and free yourself from distractions. Limit yourself to 3-5 statements to start – you can add more later. Remember, it is the start that stops most people, so take the initiative and get started NOW!

CAIN'S COACHING POINT:
CONFIDENCE CONDITIONING WORKSHEET

What do you want to change?

_____ _____

Describe the way it is right now:

_____

Why is it a problem?

_____

How do you feel about the way it is?

_____

Describe your own behavior(s) that you want to change:

_____

What are your deepest beliefs about this situation? Be honest with yourself:

_____

Describe the way it will be after the change(s) you seek (use present tense):

_____

Describe the way you will behave to generate the result you want (use present tense):

_____

What beliefs will you need in order to support these new behaviors (use present tense)?

_____

How will you feel when you bring your vision into reality? What is the personal value for you?

_____

SAMPLE CONFIDENCE CONDITIONING STATEMENTS

If they accurately express your own goals and feelings, use these examples as written, or use them as models for creating your own powerful confidence-0conditioning statements. Remember, you do not have to confine yourself to just personal and athletic-specific confidence-conditioning statements; imagine growth in any area of life you choose.

PERFORMANCE CONFIDENCE-CONDITIONING STATEMENTS

During daily performance, confidence-conditioning statements become simplified statements for more memorable self-talk. The requirements for these statements are reduced to reflect the importance that they be present tense, positive, and emotional. All other requirements, however, continue to remain relevant. When you are getting ready to take on your day, use these confidence-conditioning statements to maximize your positive mentality.

SAMPLE PERFORMANCE STATEMENTS

1. I command confidence.

2. I trust in my abilities to live a life of excellence.

3. Today is mine. I own this.

4. I will be the hardest worker in every room I am in.

5. I have put in the preparation and I am ready to lead.

6. Stay in control, baby – ANGER is only one letter away from Danger!

7. Let the negative go and the positive grow.

8. My decisions will determine my destiny.

9. Dominate the Day!

10. I am the best Athletic Administrator in the state.

Whenever you read one of your confidence-conditioning statements, pause for a moment to picture and feel that statement as it if were happening now. Consciously use the self-talk voice within your head to read and recognize the meaning of the statement.

Confidence is essential to the generation of a positive mentality. During each day and in the heat of battle, you must be confident in your ability to perform, and trust that all your preparation will pay off. This practice of confidence conditioning not only helps you harness your self-talk voice, but it also builds internal confidence, so that when the moment of truth arrives, you will believe in yourself and know that, when all is said and done, you gave yourself the best chance for success. Thus, the process of building confidence will create the positive mentality necessary for success in your pursuit of excellence.

CAIN'S GAME PLAN:
I personally set my confidence-conditioning statements in the Reminders app on my iPhone so that they pop up at specific times during the day or when I leave or arrive at specific locations.

What confidence-conditioning statements, when read on a daily basis, will help you increase your confidence and increase your positive mentality?

_____

_____

_____

_____

_____

_____

_____

CAIN'S COACHING POINT:
Earlier in this manual, we talked about your core values. How are you doing with living out those core values? Are you still setting weekly goals? Your chances for success significantly increase through the simple practice of setting daily goals. Remember, focus on the next 200 feet, working towards improvement and focusing on what you want, not on what you are trying to avoid.

THE CONFIDENCE RESUME AND LIST OF WINS

Another strategy for creating a positive mentality and conditioning yourself to be more confident is to make a confidence resume and list of wins. The confidence resume and list of wins is an activity in which you identify all of the wins you have had in your career – wins both on and off the field. The purpose of the confidence resume is to facilitate the development of greater confidence in yourself and your performance by listing all the qualifications that justify why you deserve the outcome you desire.

By nature, we as human beings beat ourselves up when we fall short of our goals and briefly celebrate our wins before we focus on what's next. For example, when you graduated from college, did you really enjoy and take confidence from the body of work you just completed, or were you focused on getting that first job out of school? When you were a child and learned how to ride a bike, did you take confidence from ditching the training wheels, or did you focus on going further and faster? Listing all of your wins will help you to see the amazing body of work you have done over time, and will allow you to have a resource you can review to help build the mental muscle of confidence.

Your confidence resume and list of wins should include anything and everything that, when reviewed, helps you feel empowered and confident. The confidence resume and list of wins should be extensive and ongoing. Like climbing the Mountain of Excellence, the confidence resume and list of wins has no finish line. Your choices can focus on your personal and professional skills. They may include previous results, quality preparation, great teammates, books you have read, people you have met, places you have been, wins you have had on the field, coaches you have played for, or doing what was uncomfortable such as asking someone out on a date and celebrating that she said yes, or that you mustered up the courage to ask even though you were turned down. (Her mistake and you learned that you need a refined process). Instead of focusing on the no, focus on the process that you asked. **_Remember, you will never get anything in life that you don't ask for._**

CAIN'S GAME PLAN:

Get started with your confidence resume and list of wins. What are some of the wins you have had in your life that you may have overlooked?   Simple wins such as how you handled a difficult decision, performances that stand out or positive experiences that you have had in life:

_____

_____

_____

_____

_____

_____

_____

Filling out the confidence resume is beneficial for Administrators because it forces individuals to identify the work they've done and the preparation they've put into the development of their craft. This exercise can provide either a confidence boost or a look at a sobering reality. Even if the resume shows you have a lot of work to do, it is important to maintain a positive mentality by realizing you are on the right path and that the resume has given you the constructive criticism you need to get started on your journey. *Remember, it is the start that stops most people.*

CAIN'S COACHING POINT:
In my work with administrators, coaches and athletes, even the best on the planet can struggle with developing their confidence resume. That struggle is exactly why we need to have the confidence resume in our arsenal as we climb the Mountain of Excellence. Confidence is fragile, and every time you review your confidence resume, it will be the equivalent of lifting weights for your confidence and belief.

You must do a little a lot to obtain the mental muscles you are looking for.   Just as physical muscles take time and effort to develop, so do your mental muscles of confidence.

After you have written out your confidence resume and reasons to believe, post them where you will see them on a daily basis. I have my list in Evernote (computer app) and review it each morning as part of my daily routine. Having this document visible will give you confidence by seeing that you have reasons to believe in yourself. Some teams I work with will create a confidence resume for the season, and review it before each game to remind the team of the hard work and preparation they have invested so that they should have confidence.

This daily action is like strength and conditioning for your mental game. Through the repetitious acknowledgement of your reasons to be confident, you will steadily build a stronger, more confident mentality. During competition, this should be reason enough to stay positive while you embrace the adversity that administration brings every day.

SOURCES OF CONFIDENCE

Confidence conditioning will improve positive self-talk, and the confidence resume will supplement your belief in yourself and a positive mentality. Both techniques of confidence building rely on a solid base of preparation. True and authentic confidence comes from the combination of actions an individual takes in preparation for performance. Confidence comes from these four key areas:

1. Physical preparation – the BST (Blood, Sweat, and Tears)

2. Positive self-talk & confidence conditioning

3. Performance routines you have to keep you consistent

4. Mental imagery of you performing at your best

There is no substitute for smart, hard work.   The consistent implementation of effective mental conditioning with your physical conditioning will give you the biggest confidence boost. Physically, you would never do strength and conditioning once a week or once a semester and expect to get any stronger. The same rules apply to mental conditioning, and by integrating it into your physical conditioning, you get the most out of mind and body. Strengthening and conditioning to enhance your mental confidence is obtained by doing a little a lot, not a lot a little. Every time you grind it out in practice and give that extra effort, and every time you take the opportunity to reflect on your confidence-conditioning statements and your confidence resume, you build the mental muscle of confidence.

Conditioning self-confidence is all about building a positive mentality. When it comes down to your performance, all you can do is rely on your preparation and execute in a manner that gives you the best opportunity for success. You cannot control anything else. You must strive for excellence in all things, to give yourself the peace of mind that you have done your best to give your best; the rest will fall into place.

KEEP YOUR CONFIDENCE HONEST
HAVE AN ACCOUNTABILITY PARTNER

A great way to keep your confidence honest is through the utilization of an accountability partner(s). The administrative situations that are on our radar are with people who are very near to us, and our vision and confidence get clouded. Your accountability partner can help clear the fog and point you in the right direction, for they are removed from the situation and see it crystal clear. This may be an acknowledgement that you're doing things right and to keep going, or will acts as a GPS device tell you to re-route. Developing these relationships will keep you in check to ensure your moving forward towards personal and professional excellence.

When it comes to confidence, there are many different ways for administrators to keep each other accountable. Feel free to arrange whatever methods you feel will serve you best. One great way to keep your confidence honest is for your accountability partner to ask you questions about your confidence whenever you see each other or through email/text messages. As professionals, if you see each other at a meeting or exchange an email update, ask "Can you tell me two things on your confidence resume?" "What are three of your confidence-conditioning statements?" If you do not respond within a few seconds or reply immediately upon reading (less than 2 minutes, right?!) then you know you are not reviewing and giving enough focus to your mental conditioning techniques.

During correspondence with the administrators I work with, the question I ask all the time is, "What are you working on today to get better?" If they cannot answer me quickly, they have not properly prepared for the objectives of their day. They are not present and are not getting the most out of their time at practice that day. They are not building mental confidence and are not building the positive mentality necessary for performance excellence. They are simply going through the motions.

> "You are capable of 20x more than you think you are."
>
> **_Mark Divine_**
> **_Navy SEAL Commander_**

FAILURE IS POSITIVE FEEDBACK

In your pursuit of excellence, you will experience failure. This is a fact. Nothing worth having comes easily, and no success story is created without trials and tribulations to overcome. Accept failure as an inevitable part of your journey, and learn to view failure as positive feedback.

Failure is actually the most effective form of positive feedback. Failure provides you with the most direct and honest insight into why and how something has gone wrong. If you are trying to accomplish a task and are giving it your best effort, exercising various techniques, but are failing, then you are receiving positive feedback from the task on what not to do. This is when you should become fascinated, not frustrated, and realize that, with each attempt, you are exposing the details that will lead you to success.

Remember the prophecy of thoughts, and how your positive or negative thoughts manifest through actions and outcomes. Be positive. Be confident. **_Confidence is a choice._** Challenge your limitations and move beyond your mistakes and shortcomings by learning from them. *In life there are winners and learners.* The quicker you make mistakes and learn from them, the quicker you move beyond them and the more prepared you are for the next 200 feet. Choose to be a learner, not a loser. Get better, not bitter. Accept failure as positive feedback.

CAIN'S COACHING POINT:
It is important to have the capacity to distinguish when you are getting closer to success and when you are moving further from it. Be sure to ask for advice or counsel when necessary, but be aware that this is your journey. Also, remember that sometimes, when the accomplishment you desire feels far away, it actually may be waiting right around the corner.

THE THREE MAGIC LETTERS – YET

When you experience a disappointment and the result you worked so hard to achieve falls beyond your reach, there is a three-letter word to keep your positive mentality – "YET." You can turn statements of failure into goal-setting exclamations by adding this simple three-letter word. This word will turn negative comments around and change your attitude, confidence and perspective. When you notice you are telling yourself (self-talk) that you cannot do this or that, add the three magic letters "Y-E-T" to the end of your sentence.

I am not as organized with my time as I want to be... YET.
I cannot maintain the high energy levels that I want to... YET.
I do not exercise daily as a part of my routine... YET.
We didn't win the championship... YET.

By adding "YET" to the end of your sentence, you leave the door to your mental hall of excellence open, as opposed to slamming the door in your own face.

YET is also an acronym for Your Energy Talks, referring to the influence of your energy on yourself, your department and your goals. When the mood is down and thoughts are negative, use this acronym to remind yourself or others to change the outlook of the situation. Disappointments will occur in your performances, but treat failures as positive feedback and learning opportunities to work smarter and harder, and keep a positive mentality.

POSITIVE ENERGY IS CONTAGIOUS

Energy is contagious. Is yours worth catching?

People subconsciously take cues from others to gauge their own feelings. You probably know when your friends and teammates aren't feeling 100 percent even before they tell you, maybe even before they are aware of it. You definitely know when people are feeling great, because they often exude an aura of positivity that is difficult to ignore. Whether through an outward expression of body language or just feeling a vibe, humans are exceptional at interpreting moods. For better or worse, we are so proficient at detecting moods that we often subconsciously take direction from them and mimic that energy in our own actions. The importance of energy in performance should be quite clear.

If energy is contagious, it is obvious you should make that energy positive. Brain research states that the strongest emotions in a group are passed along to others in a span of 7 seconds. You have the responsibility to be the tone setter. *As your school's Athletic Administrator and school leader, your energy is THE MOST CONTAGIOUS*.

"Keep your thoughts positive because
your thoughts become your words.

Keep your words positive because
your words become your behavior.

Keep your behavior positive because
your behavior becomes your habits.

Keep your habits positive because
your habits become your values.

Keep your values positive because
your values become your destiny."

Negative energy is simply counterproductive and detracts from gaining momentum for forward progress. A positive attitude when facing the challenges and obstacles of practice or competition goes a long way. Attitude reflects leadership. If you perform with a positive attitude and bring positive energy on a daily basis, the atmosphere of your staff and working environment will begin to reflect your commitment to positive energy. Therefore, if energy is contagious for producing attitudes and attitudes reflect leadership, then leadership, too, is contagious. As you perform, make a concerted effort to build a team of leaders by bringing positive energy to the table.

GET BIG

The term GET BIG refers directly to body language in relation to peak performance. It means to convey a big, confident body language. Walking down the hall, on the floor of the weight room, on the field or into your office, your body language is an expression of yourself and conveys a message to those around you.

What happens physiologically and psychologically as you GET BIG is that your brain and body will start to release chemicals that will make you feel more confident. You will start to come up with reasons why you should feel more confident, and you will become more confident. Psychology and physiology form a two-way street. You will affect your physical performance by how you think and talk to yourself, and you will affect your psychology by how you carry yourself physically, all the while reinforcing a positive self-image.

I have found that it is easier to act yourself into a way of thinking than it is to think yourself into a form of acting. You must practice GETTING BIG by consciously walking BIG, and reinforcing confidence by self-talking BIG. GETTING BIG will help you to find the confidence you need to perform at your best. One team I worked with that won an NCAA National Championship understands the importance of GETTING BIG and uses signs of success in their facility and locker room to remind them of this key peak performance principle.

CAIN'S COACHING POINT:
Where will you hang a GET BIG sign so you can see it each day?

REALISTIC POSITIVITY

A positive mentality alone will not grant you performance excellence. Do not get carried away with the thought that a positive mentality is the sole element of success, *because positivity alone will get you nowhere – you must still take massive action*. A positive mentality is, however, essential to the development of a present-moment focus on the process and your overall perception of performance and life.   Positive people do better in the face of adversity, and in the position of Athletic Administrator, there is plenty of adversity.

CHAPTER #4 REVIEW

- Thoughts manifest through actions and affect outcomes.

- A positive mentality makes a significant difference between educational self-improvement and self-stagnation, being bored.

- Defeat limiting beliefs with a positive mentality.

- Keep a positive self-image.

- Self-talk is a reflection of self-image.

- Harness your self-talk through confidence conditioning.

- Your confidence-conditioning statements build a positive mentality.

- Your confidence resume facilitates development of confident performance.

- Keep your confidence honest by utilizing an accountability partner.

- Failure is positive feedback; get better, not bitter.

- Turn statements of failure into goal-setting exclamations by adding YET.

- YET – Your Energy Talks.

- Energy is contagious, so make yours positive.

- GET BIG with your body language and self-talk.

- Know that positive thinking alone will not get you anywhere. You must couple your positive thinking with massive action.

CHAPTER #5

ESTABLISHING & ENHANCING YOUR CHAMPIONSHIP CULTURE

> "Culture creates chemistry. Without culture you can't have chemistry. High achievers don't like being around people who are mediocre, and people who are mediocre don't like being around high achievers."
>
> **Nick Saban**
> **Head Football Coach**
> **University of Alabama**

Earlier in this book, we covered the concept of developing your own set of core values to apply to your life. These core values will help guide you in every decision that you make. It is the foundation of who you are and what you are about. These deep-rooted values will leave a long-lasting image of your legacy. When your time on this planet has come to an end, the conversations held at your funeral will be based upon your commitment to those values, and every person will have been impacted by the collection of your todays.

Sportscasters often speak about a coaching tree, showing how one head coach has helped impact the careers of those who served as assistants under him/her before branching out to become head coaches themselves. You are doing the same thing right now with your work. The Excellence Tree you are building will allow those who come in contact with you to take the lessons and create their own sections of people in order to lead. The impact of your own life and the numbers affected directly or indirectly could fill up gymnasiums, arenas, and stadiums.

As a Daily Dominator and a person who aims to live an uncommon life, your role of Athletic Administrator in the development of your school's core values is crucial to the success of your department. Common measures of success are: wins, championships, all-state players or coach-of-the-year recipients, just to name a few. The public will measure success by the outcomes and not the process, because in most instances, the process is not visible to them. Developing a Championship Culture will help bring the process to light, and will give everybody who is associated with your school a mission. In the same way, you do not want to leave any doubt in people's minds about the life you live; you do not want to leave any doubt about the life your department is living.

CHAMPIONSHIP CULTURE

Define culture in your own words and explain why it is so important.

Culture is the life force of your organization. It is the humming or buzzing feeling that echoes throughout your hallways. Culture will impact all decisions and will affect how everything is done. This is reflected in the actions of the organization's members and the impact made on following the mission.

For years, organizations have created mission statements which look really good in a pamphlet or a sign on the wall, but very few in the organization outside the offices of those in charge know what that mission statement is. It is often a broad statement outlining the purpose of the organization. It misses being most effective in producing the wanted results, however, because it is hitting with a shotgun shell instead of a bullet. Hitting a pinpoint target instead of a spread of pellets gives a clearer sense of direction and purpose.

You might be reading this and thinking, "We have a winning culture and our programs are trying to make better people through athletics. Athletics teach life lessons, and we want them to develop the skills necessary for them to be successful after high school." If you think this way, great! If you are more like long-time Raider owner Al Davis' philosophy of, "Just win baby", know that winning as a sole mission is a lot like deodorant – it just covers up that which stinks. If you were to take the winning away, all of the problems would be exposed. Having a Championship Culture is not dependent upon wins, talent level or schedule, but on the process of becoming more so that your programs play at their best when it means the most and have the tools necessary to do it.

Legendary coach and master of the mental game Pat Summitt once said, "You can't just put people in a room and call them a team. They must work at it on a daily basis. They must have a set of values that dictate behavior." Coach Summitt's insight is perfect for what we will do in this chapter. We are going to establish how to launch this foundation within your own organization. This is something that takes work and is a process in and of itself. This has to be taught and has to be grown. Rome was not built in a day, and things that are built fast are not built to last. You have invested your time into this book, and for that you are not just IN but INTO doing what it takes to make your school better. Here's how we do it intentionally and not by chance.

CULTURE TEST

Each organization has a set of traits and characteristics that are consistent with how it operates. Here is the first test on whether or not you have a definable Championship Culture. If you were to ask every coach within your athletic department to list 5 traits of what it means to be a _____ (insert your mascot here), how many answers would you get?

There would be some descriptors that align with what one other coach would say, but you would get widespread responses from those within your department. These traits are all valuable for determining what needs to be done to get everybody sharing the same vision, moving your organization in the direction you wish to go.

I was working with a school in the Midwest on this same concept, gathering background information on what each individual coach thought about their athletic department's core values. This was a successful school with an energetic Athletic Administrator and passionate coaches. I asked for each of them to provide 3 values they believe the department was about. In a room of 30 coaches, we received 42 different responses!

The laughter and nervous facial expressions that ensued gave them a clear picture of their current reality. The department was operating on principles of being a decent human being, guidelines that most humans will follow in order to impact the lives of those they serve. However, they quickly realized that, even though the 42 responses received were all fabulous, this was a reality check on what needed to happen to get all 30 coaches on the same page.

THE CULTURE DEVELOPMENT PROCESS

Throughout this course of action, we are going to examine the steps necessary for you to impact your department on a different level, a level based upon process and excellence. As I mentioned earlier, this is going to take time, energy, and commitment if you want to enact change in a big way. I can promise you that it will be worth it, because you will be creating a system that can withstand the test of time and will be a foundation that is felt by all stakeholders in your school: the coaching staff, the teachers, the students, the support staff, the administration, the parents, and the community. This is not a quick fix or a flash in the pan – this is a lifestyle.

The following steps can initially take place during a staff meeting or workshop time that will be facilitated by 'you, the Athletic Administrator. The #1 complaint I heard during my time as a physical education instructor and Athletic Administrator was the pointless repetition of Professional Development. Complaints were that it wasn't important or that it was a waste of time because it was never used or re-visited again.

The body of work that will be completed here is ongoing and constant. You as the Administrator have to lead! William Arthur Ward, the original inspirational writer, said, "The mediocre teacher tells. The good teacher explains. The superior teacher demonstrates. The great teacher inspires." This is your time to be great, to apply the lessons learned in the process of becoming a better version of you to create a better version of a department.

THE FIVE STEPS TO CREATING A CHAMPIONSHIP CULTURE

1. Identify the shared values of the program/organization.

Poll each of your coaches with the following question using a Google Form, email response or pen and paper if working together in the same place:

List three character traits or values that you believe MUST be the focus of our athletic department character education program to give ourselves the best chance for success in all sports and to best prepare our athletes for success after HS. Examples of character traits and values are words like Toughness, Focus, Integrity, Respect, etc.

After all of the responses have been received, create a list of all of them, even if they have been repeated. What you are looking for here is pattern and frequency from the group. This first step is building a shared vision by all. Creating a shared vision gives each coach a sense of ownership. New initiatives fail because they are handed down as a mandate, creating separation and achieving the opposite of what was intended. A shared vision creates camaraderie and growth in personal and professional relationships.

Now that you have a list of responses, tally the most common responses listed by the group. Some might be different words to describe the same thing, for example, hard work, work ethic, and heart are all measures of the same thing. You will need to decide which word to use to express the trait you want to be displayed.

At the schools I work with, I have found that organizing the words to fit an acronym, a hand signal or an easily-memorized structure is most effective in establishing these traits. The mascot is the best, because that is who you are and what people cheer from the stands. Whether you are a Tiger, Bear, or Ram, the most common responses can be tailor-made to your staff's liking. Here are a few examples on the application of this method:

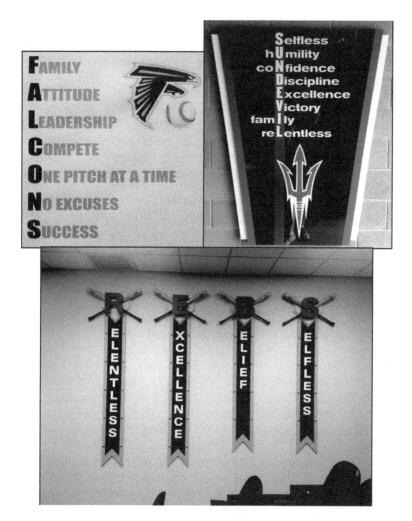

2. Define what the values mean inside your organization.

Putting definitions to each word helps to increase the level of understanding associated with the trait. Throughout this process, we are adding greater meaning and emotional response. Targeting the heart of the individual will prevent this from being a one-time deal before it fades from existence. You will facilitate the discussion on how each trait is defined for YOUR school and department.

Central Springs High School in Manly, IA are the Panthers. They created a Championship Culture with the following traits and definitions. The 25 coaches helped develop this model from 29 different responses, and settled on the definitions through a group brainstorming and idea-sharing setting.

Purpose - We will have a plan and the reasons why.
Accountable – We will do what we say we will do.
Next Play – Toughness to overcome adversity.
Together – We over me for together we are more.
Habits (of Excellence) – Consistent daily actions to desired outcome.
Energy – Positive energy giver.
Respect – Treat others how they want to be treated.
Success – Giving yourself best chance after HS career.

Once the traits and definitions have been established as a shared vision by the coaching staff, you have condensed, consolidated and focused the original spread of data points into a single, concise, focused target that will influence how everything is done within your department.

3. Describe what the values look like in action in the key areas.

Schools have different settings where your Championship Culture can be displayed, and you will have to help facilitate the areas that are of the highest value. Pick 4-5 areas that are labeled as the most important and what that value in action looks like.

Common areas for athletic programs are: in the hallways, in the classroom, in practice, in the weight room, in competition, in the community. Once you have determined which 4-5 to sharpen your focus, apply your Championship Culture traits and definitions to those areas.

For example, the Flower Mound HS Baseball in Texas has a Jaguar mascot. They chose a culture of B.I.T.E., which stands for Belief, Integrity, Toughness, and Excellence. What does Belief look like in the classroom, in the weight room, in competition, and in the community? What does Integrity look like in the classroom, in the weight room, in competition, and in the community?

Applying the concepts to the different areas gives a set of standards for coaches, athletes and parents associated with that program to follow. Standards are better than rules; the old adage states that "rules are meant to be broken," whereas standards are meant to be lived up to.

4. Assess how you are living the values.

Personal reflection upon each of these areas will lead to the truth about your current reality and the culture that is being put into action. One of the biggest mistakes that individuals can make is turning a blind eye on what is actually happening vs. what you think is happening. **We cannot change what we are not aware of.**

You will be strong in some areas and weak in others. Commit to improving one of your weaknesses and then advance to the next. As mentioned earlier, change and improvement do not happen the way they should because, once the motivational muscles kick in, too many things to change are tackled at the same time. You cannot successfully work on improving three items without fizzling out in the long term, because the work becomes too difficult to maintain.

What are the ways we can assess how we are living the values of our program?

1. Create a Google Form or online survey to send to your coaching staff that outlines the strengths and areas needing improvement of the core values.

2. Rank each of the values from 1-10, from lowest (1) to highest (10). Once these values have been assessed, use the STOP-START-CONTINUE method of evaluation to activate the process of improvement.

To help you get closer to a 10, what must you START doing?

_____

_____

To help you get closer to a 10, what must you STOP doing?

_____

_____

To help you get closer to a 10, what must you CONTINUE doing?

_____

_____

This method is self-generated and will allow you to look inward with full honesty. This information can be taken to the large group setting with your coaching staff to facilitate discussion on how your school is meeting the values established in your Championship Culture.

3. *Three Sides of the Triangle*

How You See Yourself

How Others See You
How You Want to Be Seen

This is one of my favorite exercises, because it is a combination of your own thoughts about your program and the outcome you are striving to reach. The other component of this requires full transparency – you are going to ask your peers from other schools about their view of your school. This could be your Accountability Partner whom you know will tell you the truth, or colleagues from your conference who regularly see how your teams perform. Reading these responses can be uncomfortable, but doing so will allow you to see clearly through the lens that others are looking through in order to help diagnose the areas needing to be improved.

Remember that measurement is motivation, and true assessment aims to obtain data that can provide your group with the direction where to go. University of Michigan Head Baseball Coach Erik Bakich said it best: "*If you don't have numbers that you use to measure your performance and measure your progress, you are fooling yourself. Data doesn't lie. We need more evidence, not more emotion. Evidence and data clear up the picture, emotion clouds reality.*"

5. Create a Growth Plan

Now that you have *Identified* the values of your program, *Defined* each of them, *Described* what these values look like in each of your key areas, and *Assessed* how you are living each of the values as a department, the final step is to *Create* a growth plan on how you can improve upon the needed areas.

Two different mindsets either allow you to reach your goals and potentials or cause you to fall short. They are a fixed mindset or a growth mindset.

A fixed mindset is that you are the way you are, and no matter how hard you try or the effort you give, you will never be good at this skill. An example of this would be math with young people. They will state, "I'm not good at math," as if they were born without the math gene, and no matter what they do, they will never become good at math. What keeps them from improving has little to do with their ability and more to do with their attitude and perception of the task at hand.

A growth mindset is that you can improve in any area of your life by having the correct plan and following that plan on a daily basis. Yes, things may be more difficult in some areas than others, but you are in control of your process, which will give you a greater chance to reach your desired outcome. To use the math example, a student could have difficulty in this subject, but the statement, "I'm not good at math... YET" becomes a dynamic statement indicating it is still in progress. The end result has not yet been attained, and is a matter of improvement, not a lack of genes.

When developing your program's growth plan, application has to start at the individual level. Every person within your program and department has to take ownership of making himself or herself better within the specific area of need. This has to be measured on a daily basis. If you are not growing, you are dying. If you fail to water a newly planted tree in your back yard, it will not get the nutrients it needs and it will die. The same rules apply here with your culture and growth plan: when you supply water daily, you will give it the nutrients needed to facilitate growth and life.

What are 1-2 ABSOLUTES that you must take on to close the gap from where you are to where you want to be?

_____

_____

REINFORCING YOUR CHAMPIONSHIP CULTURE

You will be investing a great deal of time on the first two steps in the beginning year or years, working to establish the values, assessments, and growth plans. Your Championship Culture takes a consistent approach over time in order to see results. Your role as Athletic Administrator and Champion for Change is increasingly important now, because reminders to your coaching staff on the importance of this culture, and the methods of delivery, have to come from you.

The Athletic Administrator position is viewed as one of power and position. Many feed off this and feel they are making decisions to display their authority. We must strive for more than just making decisions and being the one in charge. You are responsible for the growth and development of the coaches on staff, the athletes wearing your school's colors and the fans who cheer them on. Authority has negative feelings associated, while leadership brings the positive energy needed to help everybody feel they are a part of something bigger than themselves.

To enhance your Championship Culture, here are a few strategies used by Athletic Administrators.

- *Daily and Weekly Emails*: outline one specific character trait of your Championship Culture and how it can be displayed in each of your key areas.

- *Challenge Coins* bearing your Championship Culture can be given to coaches and athletes to put in their pocket as a reminder of who they are as a member of your athletic department.

- *Signs of Success:* colorful and powerful signs in classrooms, gyms, the weight room, locker rooms, etc. that outline your Championship Culture to motivate and inspire.

- *Culture Cards:* a business card for coaches and athletes to put in their wallet to outline their purpose as a member of the athletic department and the daily goals of living a life of excellence.

- *Development of a Creed or Statement of Belief*: a statement that stems from your Championship Culture values and becomes similar to a pre-game prayer or mindset-creating series of statements.

"The secret to success is good leadership, and good leadership is all about making the lives of those around you better."

Tony Dungy
Former NFL Super Bowl Champion Coach & Author

CULTURE OVER SCHEME

What you do within your athletic department to reach the goals you have set has to be driven by the culture created. This is a lifestyle that will be felt by all who are associated with your school. Athletic Administrators often speak of their time being eaten up by "constantly putting out fires." Your role is not to be a fireman, jumping from one problem to the next. Your role is like Smokey Bear, working with passion to "prevent fire." Having a Championship Culture gives you a framework in which to operate to make a positive impact on those whom you serve. This does not mean it will be easy and without problems. This job will never be without its share of issues. When these issues come to light, however, you can pinpoint why things must be done by those within your department according to the culture and shared vision.

You have got to fight like a maniac to maintain your culture and not let it be destroyed by torch-bearers looking to cause chaos. Your strength will be challenged daily in your role as Athletic Administrator, sometimes more days than others. The focus on developing a Championship Culture is that now you have a purpose and vision in which to operate and not just a tedious job where you are managing the day-to-day operations. Things will be happening now with intent; decisions will be made from principle rather than preference.

The culture at your school has to be lived and breathed by you, the Athletic Administrator. You must model your core values in action. The fruits of your labor and of those on staff will create an environment that is built on excellence and achievement. This worthwhile endeavor will create growth systems for your coaches and athletes that will impact the outcomes and build winners in and out of the competitive arena.

CHAPTER #5 REVIEW

- Five steps to establish and enhance a Championship Culture:

  1. Identify the values of your Championship Culture.

  2. Define what the values of your culture mean.

  3. Describe what the values of your Championship Culture look like in action in the keys areas of your program.

  4. Assess how you are living the Championship Culture in all key areas.

  5. Create a growth plan to become more in the key areas.

- University of Michigan Head Baseball Coach Erik Bakich said it best: "*If you don't have numbers that you use to measure your performance and measure your progress, you are fooling yourself. Data doesn't lie. We need more evidence not more emotion. Evidence and data clear up the picture, emotion clouds reality.*"

CHAPTER #6

BUILDING BETTER RELATIONSHIPS

> "Almost everything in leadership comes back to relationships. The only way you can possibly lead people is to understand people. The best way to do that is to get to know them better."
>
> ***Mike Krzyzewski***
> ***Head Basketball Coach***
> ***Duke University***

There is no other person within the school system who has more potential for impact than the Athletic Administrator. Not only does this ring true due to the leadership status and role within the school, but you are also entirely dependent upon others to complete the tasks necessary to be successful. There is, as well, an increasing number of people who depend upon you for their success.

The Athletic Administrator is in a constant state of building new relationships and growing existing relationships. In life, relationships cannot be merely maintained – they are either growing or dying. Some people in your life require more time and energy than others, but it is crucial that you invest in the right relationships that will foster growth in your personal and professional life.

This chapter will focus on how to enhance the relationships you have with those people in your life, and how to effectively meet their needs as well as your own individual needs. As mentioned throughout this book, you have been blessed with 86,400 seconds in your day to attack your goals and live a life of purpose. We need others in our life to reach the goals we set. Every one of us is standing on the shoulders of giants who have come before us. We cannot lose sight of how our lives have been positively influenced by so many others to reach the point we are today, and the duty that we have to continue to share the gifts that we have been given.

IT'S ALL ABOUT RELATIONSHIPS

There are many types of people that you have relationships with in your life. Some have been around for decades and others for only a few days or weeks. We take ideas, concepts, habits, and behaviors from every person who crosses our path as we continue on our journey to the summit of the Mountain of Excellence. We are learning how to or how not to at all times. Despite this personal trait absorption, you are still unique and nobody else on this planet is exactly like you.

We hold relationships with others very near and dear to our hearts. Our best memories and experiences were more than likely shared with somebody else. There is an emotional connection with others, and that can be either a positive or negative influence upon our life. It depends upon the people you choose to invest your time.

Name the 5 people in your life whom you spend the most time with.

1. _____

2. _____

3. _____

4. _____

5. _____

What benefit does each relationship bring to your life?

1. _____

2. _____

3. _____

4. _____

5. _____

What skill or traits have you taken from each relationship?

1. _____

2. _____

3. _____

4. _____

5. _____

Because our time on this planet is very limited, it is increasingly important that we choose to invest in the right relationships. The positivity and development that comes from being around the right people can have a massive impact on your success. Much like how I had to surround myself with better students in order to improve my grades, you need to surround yourself with better people in order to improve in the life you are living. The challenge is, **are you associating with people who are on the same mission as you?**

GIVERS vs. TAKERS

Billy was walking to school one bright and sunny day and was craving lemonade. He knew where a vending machine was by one of the city's playgrounds, and had just received his allowance from his dad that morning. After taking a trip through the monkey bars and down the slide, he arrived at the vending machine, thirstier than ever. Billy loved this vending machine too, because it was the only place in town where drinks were only $1. He could not wait and could already taste it.

Billy went ahead and put $1 in the machine and pressed B4, which was the proper selection for his much-craved lemonade. Nothing happened. With a confused look on his face, Billy shook the machine a little bit, hoping that the lemonade would shake loose. Still nothing. He was in a particularly good mood that day, so he sloughed it off as a miscue and tried again. He rubbed out the edges of the next $1 bill just to make sure the machine would take it. In went the $1 bill, and Billy once again selected B4 and waited anxiously for his lemonade to drop down. Just as had happened once before, no lemonade came.

Billy felt his blood boil. He was frustrated and shook the vending machine with all his might. He was going to be late for school and could not believe this was happening to him. He checked the power, for maybe there was a glitch in the system. The power was just fine and it showed all signs of working as it should. Man did he want that lemonade!

He then remembered that he had some change in his backpack and thought that maybe there was something wrong with the dollar bill part of the machine so it did not pick up that there was money being given. Surely coins would work. He found $1 in change and entered the coins slowly into the slot, just to make sure that the machine would take his precious money. After each coin had been entered, he once again pressed B4 and stared at the lemonade, willing it to drop. Nothing.

There's no way! Billy could not believe that he was getting robbed from this thing. It now has $3 of his money and still no lemonade. What the heck is wrong with this thing?! Billy was as determined as ever to get this much-desired lemonade. He repeated this entire process two more times, still getting nothing in return. A dejected little boy had just burned through his allowance in search of lemonade, and the machine yielded nothing in return. He ran off to school hoping to show up on time, and vowed never to return to that machine again.

How many times in your life have you invested your precious "money" (time, energy, and attention) to "vending machines" (people) and received nothing in return?

Many of you, while reading this story, would have walked away after $1 or maybe even $2, because that would have been a waste of your money. You might have even tracked down the company to get a refund! Yet people continually find themselves giving time, energy, love, and attention into people who give nothing in return. They are the takers. Takers are "negaholics" and energy vampires who suck the life out of you. They have you hooked because you think that the more time, the more attention and the more energy you give to them, that they will begin to show that in return. Yes, every once in a while they will give something back, and that's how they have you hooked. The takers are banking on your giving them whatever they need to get what they need. It is a dangerous relationship and unhealthy for your personal development and mental health.

Givers are the ones who will reciprocate the love, energy, and attention back to you, often more than what you have given. These humble warriors will have your back and support you through your life, to give you exactly what you need when you need it. The givers are the life force behind successful people; they help you reach new heights.

Who are the Takers in your life?

1. _____

2. _____

3. _____

Who are the Givers in your life?

1. _____

2. _____

3. _____

Be mindful of the people in your life who seek to take, take, take. Surrounding yourself with people on the same mission as you is worthwhile, because what you bring to the table will be accepted as commonplace, and you will have an environment for growth in every aspect of your life. You will become like the five people you spend the most time with, and if you show me these five, I will show you your future. Choose wisely.

BE TRUE TO YOURSELF

When you accepted the job as Athletic Administrator for your school, you gave up a part of your private life. But let's be honest, a life of privacy and irrelevancy is not for you and not why you are reading this book. You don't want privacy. You want your daily habits and lifestyle to be broadcast to the world and to LIVE YOUR LIFE OUT LOUD.

The problem that stems from this lifestyle choice is when you try to do things to appeal to the masses and to make others like you. Be very careful with the word "like" – like is based upon feelings and as we well know, feelings are false. Our focus should be on function. If you are doing things at a high level, you will always be sneered at by low achievers. That's the way the world works. People balk at things they do not know and that which is different than their own lifestyle.

When we steer our own beliefs and core values in order for others to like us, we are going against everything we know and have learned about the mental game. This is about displaying your toughness, resolve, and strength in all things. No, you do not walk around beating on your chest chanting, "I am who I am and if you don't like it, so what! I'm going to do me!" This will quickly turn people off to you, and your message on excellence will be lost. The quiet confidence exuded on a daily basis will show others that you are a person of strong character, prepared to lead your school, athletic department, and community to new levels. You live a life out of principle, not preference. Your decisions are made out of the principles that are the core values and championship culture of your athletic program.

If you get tied up trying to focus on people liking you, there is considerable time wasted on things that are outside of your control. By having a vision for your own life and the culture you're aiming to create at your school, others will quickly see the conviction and purpose, and everybody wants to be associated with greatness. Lions do not concern themselves with the opinion of sheep. Although this can be difficult to do in the transparency of your role, when you know that what you're doing is right and aligned with your core values, you give yourself the satisfaction to continue down the path of excellence without any hesitation.

FOUNTAIN vs. DRAIN

The Fountain is always part of the answer.

The Drain is always part of the problem.

The Fountain always has a program.
The Drain always has an excuse.

The Fountain says, "Let me do it for you."
The Drain says, "That's not my job."

The Fountain sees an answer for every problem.
The Drain sees a problem for every answer.

The Fountain sees a green near every sand trap.
The Drain sees two or three sand traps near every green.

The Fountain says, "It may be difficult, but it's possible."
The Drain says, "It may be possible, but it's too difficult."

It is real simple. If you want to be a good leader and if you want people to be like you, you MUST be a fountain. Your school does not need drains. Drains only clog things up.

Do you surround yourself with more fountains or more drains?

THE RELATIONSHIP THAT MATTERS MOST

Show me a successful Athletic Administrator and I will show you a supportive spouse at home who is the rock star behind the scenes. This section in the book is built around your #1 fan and source of support – your spouse. However, this person is often neglected, playing second fiddle to email, hosting games/activities, phone calls, and commitment to the job, when this person was the one you picked out of everybody else. Balance in your life is a vital component to success as an Athletic Administrator and to building better relationships. But sometimes the most important relationship we need to be thinking about is the one we have at home. It does not matter what your mission and vision is for your place of work if your home is not in order. The highs and lows of the job will not be celebrated or rebounded from as is necessary to be successful.

Think about your most challenging coach, the one who is an energy vampire and occupies your thoughts and feelings during many occasions throughout your day. Ponder on the parent who has a view that nobody can change, and the suffering felt by the other parents in the school because that one simply won't stop. Now imagine if you spent half of the time worrying about how to improve the relationship with your spouse as you did those people. We allow people to rent space in our heads that do not deserve to be there. We become disengaged and a shell of ourselves at home because we cannot let go of the day that was just experienced. Too often we preach a life of excellence and commitment to being where our feet are, yet fail to do so in our own personal lives.

I am not here to point fingers, for this information is coming from someone who will travel 280 days out of the year away from my wife and home. However, my wife Erin is the most important person to me, the one who allows me to succeed doing what I am called to do. In no way am I able to live this life were it not for her love and support. We made a commitment to one another, and that means we are intentional in our time as husband and wife and the growth of our relationship. The same can ring true for you and your spouse. In order for that to be accomplished at a high level, you must understand what language your spouse is speaking.

THE 5 LOVE LANGUAGES

It is vital that you and your spouse are speaking each other's language within the relationship. No, I am not talking about English, Spanish, or German, but rather what each person needs when it comes to affection and love. As Abraham Maslow outlined when he created the Hierarchy of Needs, human beings require: food, water, shelter, stability, protection, intimacy, friends, achievement, and fulfillment every day. We as individuals can seek out a number of items in order to meet our needs; the need for love, affection, friendship and belonging, however, stems from the romantic relationships we all desire.

@BrianCainPeak

Marriage counselor and author Dr. Gary Chapman says in *The 5 Love Languages* that there are five primary love languages that people speak and that to fill another's "love tank," you must speak your partner's primary love language even though that is often not your primary love language.

The 5 Love Languages are:

1. Words of Affirmation
   - Use words to affirm and support others.
   - Ex: I love you, I'm proud of you.

2. Quality Time
   - All about giving the other person your undivided attention.
   - Ex: putting away your phone on a date, choosing to be with that person on purpose.

3. Receiving Gifts
   - Objects given to show appreciation.
   - Ex: flowers, event tickets

4. Acts of Service
   - Actions speak louder than words; completing tasks.
   - Ex: doing the dishes, cleaning the house, cooking dinner.

5. Physical Touch
   - Nothing speaks more deeply than appropriate touch.
   - Ex: hugs, rubbing of back or shoulders

Chapman goes on to discuss how, much like speaking languages, each of the five love languages has different dialects and different ways for you to make a quality time deposit to help fill your partner's "love tank." He writes, "I am convinced that no single area of marriage affects the rest of marriage as much as meeting the emotional need for love."

As a busy professional, I know that you understand how valuable your time together is with your spouse. Time can be limited, and you want to make the most of it. Understand that what speaks loudly and clearly to you may be meaningless to your significant other.

How would you rank the 5 Love Languages for how YOU wish to receive love?

1. _____

2. _____

3. _____

4. _____

5. _____

How would rank the 5 Love Languages for how YOUR SPOUSE wishes to receive love?

1. _____

2. _____

3. _____

4. _____

5. _____

You can take the survey online by visiting www.5lovelanguages.com

By having a clear understanding of your spouse's needs, you will be more effective in the growth of your relationship. You need to make a conscious effort to be present with your spouse when together. **Your spouse is sharing you with the world in your role as Athletic Administrator, and they deserve to have all of you there with them when together.** Marriages fail because the lines of communication close and they stop doing the things they vowed to do. When planning your day, be sure to make time for you and your spouse to reconnect, unwind, and decompress from the day, and to look forward to the day ahead.

You must be ever intentional with your time while at home. The burnout rate is so high in this job because Athletic Administrators do not have a routine for their office life separate from their home life, and they begin to blend into each other, with the home life losing out. It doesn't have to be that way! You can be phenomenal in your role as an Athletic Administrator, spouse, parent, and whatever other endeavors you wish to pursue with excellence. Invest in your relationships at home with your spouse and children, and you will find that your role of Athletic Administrator will be even more fulfilling.

SERVANT LEADERSHIP

Earlier in the book we compared the difference between manager and leader. To review briefly, a manager is one whose goal is to make sure that everybody is doing his or her job and the status quo is being maintained. The leader is on a different level and strives to inspire others to be better than they thought they could be. The problem is that many Athletic Administrators have a great number of things they would like to do that fire them up, but are too caught up in doing the things that are urgent and not those things that are important. **Activity cannot be confused with productivity.**

As your school's ultimate leader, the leadership that has to be shown is that of servant leadership. You are the only person who gets the opportunity to work directly with every staff member and employee of the school system. Nobody in your school district has a clue what it takes to do your job the way you do. You are on an island of excellence by yourself. You have a countless number of people who need you in order to be successful, and having the correct processes, systems, and structure in place to do so will allow you and your department to flourish.

Being a servant leader is not about enabling, it is about empowering. Being selfless is not thinking less of yourself, it's thinking of yourself less. Doing everything for everybody does not make you a servant leader, it makes you a martyr. Refusal to ask for help or having the attitude that "nobody can do it better than me" will lead to burn-out and burned relationship bridges. People want to be trusted and given opportunities to shine as part of a team.

When your Championship Culture has been established and your coaching staff is focused with laser intensity upon the process of what it takes to be a top-tier athletic department, all systems will be go for take-off. Your role has to be the ultimate servant leader.

For example, when you host an event, there are staff members or community members who occupy the various roles that are essential for game day operations. Here are a few examples of those roles:

- Ticket takers
- Concession workers
- Scorer's table operators
- Video crew
- Announcers
- Music performers
- Dance performers
- Custodians

There is plenty of outside help needed to fill all of the above-mentioned roles plus others that are needed for your event to be successful. Not only do you have to manage the people that make the event go, there are also those who come in from an outside group looking to fundraise, sell, or promote something within their organization, and the event held at the local school is the vehicle for them to accomplish their goals. Throw in the officials working the game, the parents in the crowd and the spectators in attendance, and you have one large stage on which to entertain. Bring it on!

You have to assume the role of Concierge and Hospitality when people enter your facilities. It's part of your job to make sure they have an outstanding experience. This is a chance for your positivity and energy to show! It is challenging when you have hosted an event 4 out of the past 5 nights, but **fake it until you make it and act differently than how you feel** so you can display the type of skills needed to be the model everyone needs to see.

Enjoy your time roaming during your pregame routines (yes, this needs to be planned out and systematic) and greeting the officials, table workers, and ticket takers. You cannot act as if they are a burden, for you need them in order for the event to go! It kills me when Athletic Administrators get frustrated when hosting tournaments, meets, or games; it is part of the job requirement and an opportunity to put your culture on display to the public. Do not be like the waitress who is angry when customers show up to eat – embrace those who step foot on your campus, and do all that you can to put on a first-class event that will leave them happy with their experience.

Servant leadership separates itself from the other types of leadership because it is centered on growth. It focuses on the growth of your student-athletes, coaches, parents, and community members. The role you play is that of a model, doing all you can to help those you serve become the best versions of themselves. By applying the principles you have learned thus far, you will be able to impact your coaches and how they live their lives, who will in turn impact the athletes and parents of their programs. It becomes a widespread positive energy takeover that transforms your school.

SUPPORT ARMY

The turnover rate the Athletic Administrator position in schools is as high as it has ever been. The world is constantly changing, and you need to stay up with the times. Athletic Administrators, I have found, are the ones who can be the furthest behind in this growth. College coaches have to stay up with the current times so that they can recruit the best athletes, which will lead to success within their sport. To be an effective administrator, you cannot have the mentality of "that's the way we have always done it." You must inspect what you expect in your department and develop the systems to achieve it.

One of the systems that will help you to maintain mental stability and allow you to maximize your daily potential is the proper utilization of your support systems, or as I like to call it, your support army.

Repeat after me: "I cannot do this job alone." You are not Superman and cannot leap tall buildings in a single bound and accomplish everything. You need help. There are so many people who are willing to assist in your job and who are waiting for you to ask. Unfortunately, many people still view asking for help as a weakness. In my early years as an Athletic Administrator, I felt that by asking others for help, I was taking the easy way out instead of doing it myself. I can tell you that it was not sustainable, and my personal self took a back seat to others and the many jobs at hand. There is too much to do, and too many other items of importance are needed from you instead of the urgent, or busy, work that occupies most of our day.

We are going to review different groups of people within your school system who can assist you in the daily activities, as well as the events that are hosted on your campus. Every person in this list is highly capable of performing any skill within your department. The time commitment is dependent upon the task, but what you are building is your Support Army and a long list of people ready and willing step up.

Administrators
(Superintendents, Principals, Associate Principals)

These are often under-utilized within school systems as a form of help during game day management. Work hard to get on the same page as an administrative team, and communicate with them what is needed for you to be successful as the Athletic Administrator. Enlist them to help with crowd management during events in outdoor facilities, and for them to take over for you when a night off is needed so you can take your spouse on a date night.

Teaching Staff (Full-time, part-time, para-educators)

Depending upon your structure in the master contract, and if teachers need to fulfill a certain requirement of work/duty obligations for the district each year, the teaching staff is an outstanding commodity. The teachers are organized, often know many of the students, and are useful for event management. They can be assigned to work the ticket booth, scoreboard operation, public address announcements or design the programs.

Secretaries

They are the most important people in the building. They know everything that happens and essentially run the school. Appreciate them for all that they do. If you are in a school big enough to have an athletic secretary, you are very fortunate. They will be able to help with budgeting, programs, emails, and phone calls. Do not miss an opportunity to show gratitude towards them and what they do to allow you to do your job at the highest level. Never skimp on Secretary's Day, their birthday, Valentine's Day, Christmas, or any time for that matter.

Custodians

These are the unsung heroes of the athletic department and too often the under-appreciated. The men and women who work hard at keeping the facilities in top shape deserve the utmost respect. As a part of your pre-season routine, outline with them what you need for each event, from bathroom walk-throughs, garbage collection, floor sweeping and hallway monitoring to setup/tear down. These people can be your best friends or your worst enemies; treat them not as a cleaning crew but as an essential part of what happens in the athletic department. Present them with any sport-related clothing you can.

Parents

There are entire books written about parents today and how to handle the challenge you are going to face. Times have changed and so has the family structure of many homes.

Parents love their kids, sometimes to a fault. You should love their kids too. Everybody has an environment they came from, and their experiences have led them into who they are today. When you really think about it, how many difficult parents are there within your district who wreak havoc upon the athletic department and school system as a whole? More times than not, you only have a handful, yet you let 20% of your parental population ruin it for the other 80% who believe in what is happening at your school.

The Championship Culture at your school is a vision shared by all. You can effectively communicate this to the parents through social media, email, newsletters, mailers, and meetings. Hold a parent meeting during orientation to talk about the culture being established at your school and how that will affect everybody and their mindset. Require each coach to hold a parent meeting before the start of the season to outline the policies and procedures of their sport and the standards to be a member of that team. Follow up with the parents throughout the year as a continuation of what is taking place.

Stop viewing the parents as a burden and look at them as an asset. You will find that there are a lot of parents who are protective of their children and want others to have their best interests in mind. What a great opportunity to display servant leadership. The parents who believe in you and your mission will do whatever task you need. Work hard at developing and building those relationships so you have them at your side when roles need to be filled.

Students

I would suggest working with your guidance counselor and principal on the implementation of a school service or athletic club program where you get to have 1-2 students with you for a certain class period during the day. These students are hand-picked by you, and will work wonders on taking care of many urgent items while you tackle the bigger important items. Assign them to print programs, set up the sound system, organize the ticket booth, deliver locker room keys and signs, etc. You can also look to the National Honor Society or Student Government to assist in your tasks as a way to gain volunteer hours.

"If you can help enough other people get what they want, you will get everything in life you want."

Zig Ziglar
Entrepreneur and Motivational Speaker

MILLER's 5 KEYS TO HAPPINESS

There are five simple rules to happiness that were shared with me by Ethan Miller, Athletic Director at Central Springs High School in Manly, Iowa. When applied, these can make a drastic improvement in your outlook on the world and how you view others.

1. Free your heart from hatred.
2. Free your mind from worries.
3. Live a simple life.
4. Give more to others than they expect.
5. Expect to get less from others.

This is a powerful concept and removes the fog from our minds, allowing us to focus on those things that really matter. The role of Athletic Administrator that you have accepted comes with a plethora of requirements that keep you from living the life you want if you allow the requirements to take hold of you.

You have chosen to live a public life where your decisions are going to be dissected and questioned by those in the media, your community, your building and office. This can cause a great deal of stress and fatigue by worrying about those things that are outside your control. When you have a values-based mission for what you are doing, you can have confidence that what you are doing is right. When doubters surface and energy vampires prey at your door, remember that being an Athletic Administrator is **what you do, not who you are.** You are more than what others make you out to be. Trust in your process of living and the direction you are leading. Nobody ever said that this was going to be easy, but they did say it will be worth it.

CHAPTER #6 REVIEW

- The 5 Love Languages
  1. Words of Affirmation
  2. Quality Time
  3. Receiving Gifts
  4. Acts of Service
  5. Physical Touch

- Ethan Miller's 5 Keys to Happiness
  1. Free your heart from hatred.
  2. Free your mind from worries.
  3. Live a simple life.
  4. Give more to others than they expect.
  5. Expect to get less from others.

- Don't confuse activity with productivity.

- Create your support army.

- Being selfless is not thinking of less of yourself, it's thinking of yourself less.

- Are you an energy giver or an energy taker?

CHAPTER #7

RECOGNIZE, RELEASE, REFOCUS

> "The secret of success is learning how to use pain and pleasure instead of having pain and pleasure use you. If you do that, you're in control of your life. If you don't, life controls you."
>
> **Tony Robbins**
> **Entrepreneur & Life Coach**

As an Athletic Administrator, stress is a very real. Employees in the school system report that they experience at least one day of high stress per week. Elevated stress levels lead to poor work performance, deterioration of relationships, and a decline in health. When not properly managed, it can lead to bigger mental health problems such as anxiety and depression.

Recognizing your physical, emotional and mental state within the context of your environment is critical to staying in control of yourself, thereby giving yourself the best opportunity for success.

As an AD, it is essential to develop a routine in which you recognize where you are mentally, emotionally and physically. Also, have a release to use when you are in a negative place so you can refocus on the task at hand and not drag negativity into your next encounter. This is will allow you to better serve the coaches and athletes in your school in the development of their own routines for mental, physical and emotional management.

This chapter will give you the skills to develop your own mental management system to keep your state of mind active and engaged in the moment as you journey up the Mountain of Excellence.

RECOGNIZING YOUR SIGNAL LIGHTS

The most challenging aspect of the mental game is learning to recognize when your performance is taking a turn for the worse, and then developing a system to make the corrections necessary to return to a place of performance excellence. As mentioned many times throughout this book, you are performing every single day. In order for you to expect top performance from others, you must be able to display this out of yourself every single day.

The recognition that you are having a performance breakdown is the primary and most crucial step in the process of living one moment at a time. Recognizing where you are – mentally, emotionally, and physically – is called your Awareness To Win. Nobody is perfect. Everybody will lose control of themselves on occasion, but it is the performer who can correct the quickest who tends to perform consistently and, ultimately, has more success.

SIGNAL LIGHTS FOR ATHLETIC ADMINISTRATORS

If you are driving a car and you come to a green light, you would naturally GO! If the light turns yellow, some of us would slow down while others would speed up, depending on where we are in relation to the light. When you come to a red light, however, you must stop or you are going to crash and burn. Now, if you are reading this chuckling to yourself about the time you ran a red light and didn't cause an accident or get caught by the police, than I am with you. However, we must caution against such consistent action – because you might run a red light once and live, but do it routinely and you will crash and burn.

OFFICER CAIN'S COACHING POINT:
"Be aware of your signal lights in administration. If you run through red lights, you will crash and burn. Live as many moments as you can in green lights to give yourself the best chance for success."

Performance awareness in administration and leadership is similar to driving a car on the road. When you have green lights (positive, confident, specific, and productive thoughts and feelings), you are in control of yourself. In performance, you encounter yellow lights (hopeful, uncertain, vague, and timid thoughts and feelings), which occur when something negative happens to take you out of a green light mentality. If your yellow lights are not recognized and addressed, you will often find yourself in red lights (negative, dejected, apathetic, and destructive thoughts and feelings). Operating in yellow or red lights is a recipe for beating yourself with poor performance, and will yield undesirable results.

The easiest way for you to think about your signal lights is this:

Green – You are giving yourself the best opportunity for performance excellence.

Yellow – You are starting to lose the mentality conducive to peak performance.

Red – You are totally out of control and it is reflecting in your performance.

The goal of all peak performers is to operate with green lights as much as possible, while focusing on the next 200 feet of the journey.

CAUSES OF YELLOW & RED LIGHTS

One thing that makes the role of Athletic Administrator so unique and special is the number of obstacles you experience on a daily basis. One of the most common causes of yellow and red lights for administrators is handling things that are outside of your control. You must be able to release your negative emotions and encounters (red lights) and not take them home with you, or vice versa. Your performance routines give you a place to go when you get into a red light and stress levels are at their max. When your day begins, yellow and red lights could result from making a mistake, a coach's criticism, fans getting on your nerves, parents filling up your inbox, or any number of other things that can become stuck in your head.

Adversity comes in all forms, physical and mental, and does not have to involve events within your environment. The world outside of your arena also can affect your performance if you are not in control of yourself. These might include that disagreement you had with your spouse last night, one of your children acting out at school, or the scheduling work you have to finish. Do not let these things distract you from your present-moment focus and peak performance mentality of being where your feet are. Focusing on what you are trying to avoid, instead of what you are trying to accomplish, is a signal that you are in a yellow or red light.

In administration, if your mind is illuminated by the red lights of a negative mentality, you are nearly guaranteed to be on the losing end. Focusing on what you are trying to avoid instead of what you are trying to accomplish is a recipe for disastrous performance in your job and in life.

THREE WAYS TO RECOGNIZE YOUR SIGNAL LIGHTS

There are three major areas where you can develop your performance awareness and learn to better recognize your signal lights. The three areas in which you can often recognize where you are mentally, physically, and emotionally are these:

1. Self-talk – What you are saying to yourself

2. Physical feelings – How you are feeling, physically

3. Situations – Circumstances that arise in your work that will trigger particular signal lights

CAIN'S COACHING POINT:
The purpose of routines is to maintain self-control and get into a green light performance mentality as often as possible.

GREEN LIGHTS – THE "CAN" MENTALITY

Green lights are an easy concept to comprehend. They represent the mentality of peak performance, where you are feeling positive and confident, focused on the present process at hand and in control of your performance thoughts and actions. Green lights are performance movers and confidence builders. One administrator I worked with referred to the green light mentality as the CAN mentality – Confident, Assertive, Number 1.

When you are confident, assertive, and number 1, you are locked into the moment and moving forward with green lights. Staying in the green light zone, you give yourself the best opportunity to have a productive day in all facets of your life.

In order to recognize when you are not in a green light state of mind, you must first recognize what signs indicate that you are in the green. The next three sections will help you use the three major areas of signal light recognition to identify your green light mentality.

GREEN LIGHTS – SELF-TALK

When you have green lights, what are you saying to yourself? Some examples could be:

1. I love this, I have the best job in the world.

2. I am living my mission and get to serve so many.

3. This is easy, I am too blessed to be stressed.

Green light thoughts are much like your confidence conditioning statements, but they are shorter and very specific to your administrative performance. They are positive, external, specific and confident thoughts.

CAIN'S GAME PLAN:
Write down your green light thoughts – what do you say to yourself when you are at your best?

_____

_____

GREEN LIGHTS – PHYSICAL FEELINGS

When you have green lights, how do you feel physically? Most administrators report:

1. I have a bounce in my step.

2. My muscles are relaxed and I have good energy.

3. I feel calm and I have big body language.

CAIN'S GAME PLAN:
Write down your green light feelings — how do you feel about yourself when you are at your best?

_____

_____

GREEN LIGHTS – SITUATIONS

What situations or actions in the classroom, the meeting room, in event management, or within the community, put you into green lights?

Most administrators report:

1. When I have had positive interactions with those I encounter

2. When I have had a good night's sleep

3. When I have my daily agenda set and it lines up perfectly

CAIN'S GAME PLAN:
Write down the situations in performance that will place you into your green light — the situations where you know you will be at your best.

_____

_____

RED & YELLOW LIGHTS

Athletic Administrators I have worked with in the past have occasionally become caught up in trying to identify whether they were in a red light or yellow light.

As the leader, I want you to be increasingly aware of your mentality and the impact that it has upon those around you. It is a fact that you do not get the luxury of having somebody to coach you up on how to return to the green light mentality you need to be at your best. This goes with the territory of the position you hold. The distinction between if you're in a yellow or red light does not matter as much. Red lights are negative thoughts, confidence cutters, and performance stoppers – and yellow lights are a sign that you are on your way to red. Green is where you want and need to be.

Thoughts become things and if you find your mindset affecting the environment around you, it needs to be addressed. Ignoring that which is happening inside of you can produce a figurative rain cloud above you. This will be disastrous to the culture you wish to create and the influence you have around each place you enter. Not only are you developing the culture

All you need to identify is whether or not you are giving yourself the green light. If you are not in the green, then recognize, release and refocus on the moment at hand. The next three sections will help you use the three major areas of signal light recognition to identify whether you are in red/yellow lights.

RED/YELLOW LIGHTS – SELF-TALK

When you have red/yellow lights, what are you saying to yourself?

Most administrators report:

1. I cannot believe people these days.

2. Why is the coach doing that?

3. Why can't I figure out how to format this document?

4. Why do I care so much?

5. I hate this damn job.

CAIN'S GAME PLAN:
Write down your red/yellow light thoughts — what do you say to yourself when you are struggling?

_____

_____

RED/YELLOW LIGHTS – PHYSICAL FEELINGS

When you have red/yellow lights, how do you feel physically?

Most administrators report:

1. I don't feel good; I feel tired and slow.

2. I feel like my heart is constantly racing.

3. I am completely unmotivated.

4. I am not making a difference here.

5. I feel like I cannot get a grip on what I'm doing.

CAIN'S GAME PLAN:
Write down your red/yellow light feelings — what do you feel physically when you are struggling on the field?

_____

_____

RED/YELLOW LIGHTS – SITUATIONS

What situations or actions in the classroom, the meeting room, in event management, or within the community put you into red/yellow lights?

Most administrators report:

1. When I fail to address a parent issue, hoping that it will go away

2. When a coach displays inappropriate conduct in public

3. When the administration makes a decision that inhibits our Championship Culture

4. When I know I could have prepared better for my day

CAIN'S GAME PLAN:
Write down what situations as an Athletic Administrator, put you into a red/yellow light and what happens when you are at your worst. What removes you from your green light mentality?

_____

_____

SIGNAL LIGHTS = PERFORMANCE CHANGE

Once you have identified your self-talk, physical feelings and the situations that put you into your green and red/yellow lights, you immediately give yourself a better chance to recognize your signal lights when they arise. If you have green lights, refocus on the next moment of your day and be present. If you have red/yellow lights, you must release before you refocus.

Remember the three steps to performance change:

1. Develop awareness of what needs to change.

2. Develop a strategy for change to happen.

3. Put that strategy into action.

A lot of administrators do not know how to make necessary mental and emotional performance adjustments because they have not developed performance awareness. Performance change is all about understanding your internal signal lights. **Mentally, what you are aware of you can control; what you are unaware of is going to control you.** This is why understanding and practicing the signal lights concept gives you the best opportunity to effectively exercise the three steps of performance change.

INVERTED U OF SIGNAL LIGHTS

Peak Performance 101 is about understanding the Inverted U.

On the North-South axis we have performance, and on the East-West axis there is intensity or focus.

How excited are you?

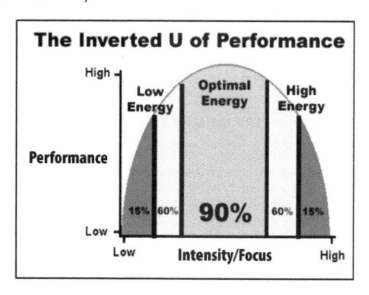

When you are not intense or focused enough, performance is low. Conversely, when you are overly intense or are too focused and trying too hard, performance is still low. This is why it is important for peak performers to maintain a consistent mental state of excellence to compete with optimal energy and perform at their best on a consistent moment-to-moment basis. The routines you have set and allowing yourself to take deep breath will permit you to manage your mental, emotional and physical self to stay in the moment and at your peak of optimal energy on the Inverted U of Performance.

This mental state of performance excellence is maintained through the adoption of performance routines that create a mental management system. A mental management routine takes you from falling anywhere on the inverted U and gives you a much better chance of consistently falling in the center, which is your optimal energy and arousal area for a peak performance, the area that some people refer to as "the zone." This routine-based mental maintenance system gives you the best chance of performing at the peak of the Inverted U and in the state where you give yourself the best chance for success.

PERFORMANCE ROUTINES

Performance routines are the life jacket of peak performance. When the pressure is on, as it usually is in Athletic Administration, you turn to your routines so that you can stay in the present moment and increase your chances of achieving performance excellence. The importance of routines to performance is a simple formula: Routines lead to consistency, consistency leads to confidence, and confidence leads to success.

CAIN'S COACHING POINT:
To be consistent over time, you must be able to describe what you do as a process/routine.

The best Athletic Administrators I have worked with have specific systems and structured performance routines that help them perform consistently over the course of the day, the specific season at hand, and the entire year. These people often stress the importance of having a focal point to turn to during pressure-filled moments. When you get distracted or you have red/yellow light thoughts and start beating yourself up, your focal point is your box of positive thoughts; they represent your checkpoint to help you slow down and get back into green lights.

RELEASE

Once you have learned to recognize your signal lights, the next step in the process is developing a release routine to help you rid yourself of the negative emotion that will slow you down.

The purpose of your release/physical routine is to help you get back in control of yourself and back into your green lights.

This release routine facilitates your transition back to a green light mentality. When you are in red/yellow lights, you must develop some sort of physical routine to help you mentally release the negative frustration. This physical action should be an expressive release to get control of your mental state and return you to the pursuit of performance excellence back in the present moment.

CAIN'S GAME PLAN:
Examples of common releases for Athletic Administrators are to clap your hands or untie and retie your shoelaces. What are physical releases you can use to help you get from red/yellow lights and back to green?

_____

_____

RELEASE YOUR MENTAL BRICKS

The reality is that at one point or another, we all make errors and mistakes or fall prey to unrealistic expectations. There is a common tendency to continue to carry mistakes and poor performances with us, resulting in a buildup of negative mental energy. Instead of beating yourself up over a poor performance, interaction or moment, you must learn to release these "mental bricks" that weigh on your mind.

If, every time you make a mistake, you were to grab a physical brick and carry that brick with you, it would weigh you down both physically and mentally. This would invariably inhibit you from performing to the best of your ability.

Now, visualize a mistake you are bitter about as a mental brick. When you carry this mistake with you, this mental brick takes the same toll as carrying a physical brick. The difference is you cannot see it because it is a weight within your mind.

In your quest for excellence, you must train yourself to release the mental bricks that threaten to weigh you down. Releasing your mental bricks relies on a process of reflection and realization followed by the release. After a mistake or a poor performance, you must thoughtfully reflect on the experience and consider how you can improve. Once you have realized what improvements can be made in your performance, you can then release the error from your consciousness and move on. The release process should happen as quickly as possible. *Releasing a negative moment and getting to the next one is a skill that must be developed through repetition.*

EXAMPLES OF PRESENT-MOMENT RELEASES

Present-moment releases should be directed at a consistent focal point. Your focal point could be an object somewhere in your office or on a part of your body. Whatever that focal point may be, when you look at it, you should take a good deep breath, get bigger with your body language and put all of that red/yellow light, negative energy and self-doubt into that focal point and let it go as you exhale.

As you transfer that energy, remind yourself to get back to the present moment and what's important now (#WIN) and return to your green light thoughts and green light/refocus routine.

An example of this might be to take off your watch, take a deep breath, and put it back on. This physical action allows you to make a mental connection to the next moment. You could stop what you're doing, pull up your socks, take a deep breath, and get back to what you were doing. In the process, you get rid of the negative thoughts and feelings and get yourself moving towards the most important moment of your day... the next one!

What you adopt for a release is entirely up to you and what that trigger does to get you back into present-moment focus. Having awareness of what is taking place inside of you, and utilizing the release to let those feelings go, will become part of your routine in your life of excellence. No matter the action, each release should consist of three parts:

1. *A physical movement*
2. *A cleansing deep breath on a focal point*

3. A verbal cue to get back to the next pitch

Here are some more examples of release routines:

You can take the keys out of your pocket and shake them to shake off the red/yellow light thoughts.

You can make a fist, and as you release your fingers, release the negative thoughts.

You can quietly use your thumbs to re-tuck the side of your shirt to sharpen up and put the red/yellow lights away.

There are hundreds of different releases you can use. The important part of the release is to be sure that you have something physical that you do, that you are taking a cleansing deep breath on a focal point, and that you have a verbal cue, all as a part of your release.

FLUSH IT

A fun way to think about releasing mental bricks is by conjuring the image of a toilet. When you have a mental brick that is in danger of putting you in red lights, you want to take this mental brick and "flush it." Once you are relieved of that mental brick, you are ready to return to the present moment in your performance.

It is inevitable, as you climb the Mountain of Excellence, that you will face forms of adversity that weigh on your mind. Do not carry these mental bricks with you on your journey. Stop routinely at your mental toilet to relieve yourself of their weight. Perform your release routine to flush away the negativity built within those mental bricks. Your mind will feel lighter and clearer, and you will be more mentally agile when you get back to your climb of living in this present moment.

REFOCUS ON TO THE NEXT MOMENT

Once you recognize your signal lights and release your red/yellow lights with your release routine, it becomes critical that you refocus back into the present moment.

Refocusing returns your mind to the next moment and pushes you towards performance excellence. One of the best ways you can refocus is to talk out loud and be involved with those around you. *When you talk out loud, you are external and present*. The tendency for the vast majority of people is to shut down and hide away. When you are quiet, you can easily get lost in your own head, thinking about the past or the future. Refocus back to the present moment – you will give yourself the best chance to perform at your best and be an energy giver.

SO WHAT! MENTALITY

Let me ask you this. Are you so fragile that everything has to go your way and zero adversity is experienced in order for you to be productive? If the answer is no, why do you get so angry when things don't go your way or there's adversity?

Refocusing, just like all mental conditioning skills, requires that your mind and body work together. If your body is trying to live in the moment and your mind is still analyzing something that happened to you three hours ago or thinking about the potential ramifications of a serious issue, your mind and body are working against each other and you lose.

You want to live in the big picture and compete in the moment. When things aren't going your way, you have got to embrace adversity. Say "So What!" **(#SW)** Let go of the past and get back to thriving in the present moment and executing the next task at hand.

"So What!" is a verbal key that you can use to help you refocus back into the present moment. This key helps you bridge from the past by saying "So What" and returns you to where you want to be in the present.

You cannot just say "So What!" with your mouth; you have to say it with your body as well. By using your physical release routine to return to the present, regardless of how you feel about the past, saying "So What!" refocuses your mind. You can then actively engage in the most important part of your performance – the next 200 feet.

In life and administration, negative things happen. Adversity is going to strike and there is nothing you can do to stop it. And why would you want to stop adversity? Adversity is a positive. Adversity is what causes you to grow. *Adversity and success are neighbors on the highway to excellence; you can't get one without the other.*

Some tragedies and some of life's unfortunate circumstances are simply outside of your control. What you cannot do is allow yourself to get caught up in a moment that has already passed. You must constantly move on to the next one. This "So What!" mentality is the hallmark of all peak performers in business, education, and athletics.

REFOCUS SIGN

When I go into the meeting rooms and offices of the athletic programs I work with, I often hang up a sign that says "REFOCUS." I teach them that when they recognize their minds starting to wander, they only have to look at the sign and refocus. Using the sign as a focal point gets them back into the next moment. This is another very simple yet highly effective tool to help you get back into the present moment.

THE RECOGNIZE – RELEASE – REFOCUS CYCLE

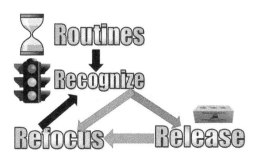

The process of the recognize-release-refocus cycle is an important one to master in your pursuit of performance excellence in athletic administration. This process is founded on an internal awareness of your signal lights, especially the ability to recognize when you are out of your green light mentality. Upon recognizing your yellow or red light state of mind, you must make a present-moment performance change by performing your release routine in order to refocus on the next moment.

This process is conceptually simple and highly effective, yet it is amazing how many neglect this cycle to maximize their performance potential.

This is one of the mental conditioning systems that separates the good and the great. If you want to consistently perform at a high level of excellence, you must learn how to recognize your signal lights, release frustration from previous portions of your day, and refocus on the present moment. Take a strong hold of the things that are within your control and let go those that are outside of your control.

CAIN'S COACHING POINT:
When you have adversity that goes against you, use the verbal release & refocus, "So What!"

A REALISTIC LOOK AT "THE ZONE"

I don't think you will ever be in green lights for an entire day. If you find yourself in "the zone," with that relaxed intensity and your green lights on steady, then enjoy the ride, baby, 'cause it doesn't last forever!

Peak performance is not about being in "the zone" all the time and having everything in the day go your way. Adversity is built into the fabric of athletics and leadership, making every day unique and full of new variables and situations for administrators to overcome.

Peak performance is about being your best when you need it the most, each and every moment of every day. It is about compensating and adjusting to the present-moment conditions of the environment you are in. It is about handling and managing pressure better than anybody. It is about rolling with the punches until you get the job done. The better your routines and the more systematic your approach, the better your chance to stay in the green lights and perform on the level of excellence one moment at a time.

Great administrators embrace adversity. They welcome it and they starve for it, because they know their ability to overcome adversity is what makes them great. The more adverse the conditions that day, the better they are, because they know they are better equipped to handle adversity than anybody else.

COMPARED TO WHAT?

When stress levels rise and yellow/red light mentality sets in, it is vital to have perspective on the situation at hand. Adversity is not easy and will never go away. The recognition system of knowing your signal lights will allow you to navigate this stress in an appropriate manner.

We have all sorts of tragedy in our world today and situations that are life-altering. Having the right perspective on the things that truly matter will help you to refocus and attack head on the issues that come at you as the AD.

When a new challenge is presented that seems to be difficult, take a hard look at the impact this situation has in the context of severity. Is the situation with the difficult parent as bad as losing your home to a fire? Is the star athlete whom you have to discipline for underage drinking right before playoffs, as difficult as it would be to lose a loved one? Is removing a rogue coach who refuses to follow a professional code of ethics as challenging as being a soldier overseas fighting for our country?

The ability to look at the big picture in the situations that arise as an Athletic Administrator will help get you from yellow/red lights and back to green lights quicker. Ask yourself this question, "Will this issue still be an issue in 5 hours? 5 days? 5 weeks? 5 months? 5 years?" The further down the question you go, the better you will get a grasp on the size of the problem by looking at it through a normal lens, not a magnifying glass.

Your strength will be challenged daily, and implementing the "So What!" and "Compared to What?" mentality to your day will keep you in green lights longer and yellow/red lights shorter. This does not mean you are downplaying or minimizing the situations, but rather looking at a situation as it is instead of how it's perceived.

CHAPTER #7 REVIEW

- The ability to recognize your physical, emotional and mental state within the context of your competitive environment is absolutely necessary.

- Green signal lights – you are giving yourself the best opportunity for performance excellence.

- Yellow signal lights – you are starting to lose the mentality conducive to peak performance.

- Red signal lights – You are totally out of control and it is reflected in your performance.

- Mastery of performance awareness is developed by understanding your self-talk, physical feelings, and how you deal with common situations during performance.

- A routine-based mental maintenance system keeps you at the peak of the Inverted U of Performance and in your best state for peak performance.

- To be consistent over time, you must be able to describe your routines as a process.

- The purpose of your physical routine and release is to help you get back in control of yourself and back into your green lights.

- Release your mental bricks by doing something physical, taking a cleansing breath, and having a verbal cue that you go to.

- All releases should be directed at a consistent focal point.

- Be sure to take a deep breath during your release.

- When you have a mental brick, relieve your mind and "Flush It."

- Refocus on WIN (What's Important Now).

- Develop a "So What!" mentality to refocus when adversity strikes.

- Use a refocus sign as a focal point.

- Peak performance is not about being in "the zone," it is about making the necessary adjustments to perform consistently at a level of excellence and to be able to compensate and adjust.

CHAPTER #8

YOUR RESPONSE-ABILITY

> "The ultimate measure of a man is not where he stands in moments of comfort and convenience, but where he stands at times of challenge and controversy."
>
> ***Martin Luther King, Jr.***

The most powerful ten-word sentence in the English language consists of only seven short two-letter words. That sentence is: **If it is to be, it is up to me.** This encapsulates response-ability.

Response-ability is taking ownership of your past, commanding your present and taking charge of your future. It is being accountable for your perspective and controlling how you choose to respond to adversity. Too many people are negatively affected by outside influences they cannot control. They respond by becoming a victim of outside factors, rather than responding to adversity by holding themselves responsible for their actions. ***Choosing your response in any situation is the greatest of all personal powers we possess as human beings.***

In this chapter, the importance of response-ability will be made clear. You will learn how response-ability makes a difference in performance, and how to begin disciplining your mind to respond to events in order to produce productive outcomes.

MAN FREEZES TO DEATH
LACK OF RESPONSE-ABILITY

In the February 1978 issue of *Success Unlimited*, psychologist Dr. Dudley Calvert tells the story of a railway employee in Russia who accidentally locked himself in a refrigerator car. Inside the car, he could not unlock the door nor could he attract the attention of those outside. Unable to escape, he resigned himself to his fate. As he felt his body becoming numb, he documented his story and his approaching death in sentences scribbled on the wall of the car.

"I am becoming colder now," he wrote. "Still colder, now I can hardly write..." and, finally, "these may be my last words." And they were.

When the car was opened upon arrival at its destination, other railway employees found him dead. Yet, the temperature of the car was 56 DEGREES! The freezing apparatus had been out of order in the car and was inaccurately stuck on 28 degrees.

There was no physical reason for his death. There was plenty of air – he hadn't suffocated. What happened was that he gave away his personal power and defeated himself by not responding appropriately to the challenges in front of him. He let the power of his mind negatively affect his reality. ***Remember, perspective is reality, and you are response-able for choosing any attitude and any perspective you want in any given situation.*** His own lack of response-ability led to his demise, a victim of his own delusion.

MAN OVERCOMES HELL ON EARTH
RESPONSE-ABILITY

In *Man's Search for Meaning*, Viktor Frankl talks about his unfathomable experience and survival of the Nazi concentration camps in World War II. Frankl, a psychologist, knew he was response-able for his mental state and his only chance at survival in his hell-on-earth conditions. He chose to search for something of value and meaning every day of his struggle.

Living in the concentration camp, Frankl discovered the Nazis could take away his family, his freedom, his food and his health, but they could not take away the last of the human freedoms: one's ability to choose his/her own attitude. Frankl realized that his ability to determine how he responded to his environment was psychological and that his human spirit was still free. With this in mind, he found daily existential meaning and purpose in aiding other prisoners by sharing the little food he did have and offering comforting words.

Unlike our man in the boxcar who went down the path of negativity, Frankl chose a path of positive empowerment. Both men had response-ability. If Frankl could survive and find meaning in the horrific experience of the concentration camps, and a man can freeze to death in a non-freezing boxcar, imagine what your response-ability can do for you. Imagine what you can endure.

Have you seen the movie *The Lone Survivor*? That movie shows what the human will can endure. Navy SEAL Marcus Luttrell demonstrates what human beings are capable of enduring and how we can be trained to do almost anything. Can you survive the perceived challenges of your everyday life and maintain a positive attitude? Absolutely! To be a peak performer, a sense of response-ability is a must.

EVENT + RESPONSE = OUTCOME

There is a simple math equation that I want you to learn and, more importantly, implement on a daily basis. This is the same math equation that the Ohio State University football team had on a spirit band they wore during their 2014-15 NCAA Football National Championship.

E [Event] + R [Response] = O [Outcome]

In life, it is not what happens to you, it is how you handle what happens to you. It is your ability to respond (response-ability) that is going to determine your outcome when adversity is thrown your way.

As a human being, YOU have the ability to respond to an event in the manner you deem appropriate. The response is your choice. Humans have the unique ability to socialize their innate responses to events with the three steps of performance improvement: (1) awareness, (2) strategy and (3) implementation of the strategy. We have previously discussed this process, and it provides an essential foundation for full comprehension of E + R = O.

We often do not have much control over the Events in our lives, but we do control our Responses. This is an empowering notion, because once you realize that you control half the equation, you recognize that you control half the outcome. If a negative event occurs and you keep a positive present-moment focus with a big-picture mentality and a "Compared to what?" perspective as your response, then you will significantly influence the outcome in your favor.

This is the process of mental conditioning that you prepare in order to thoroughly establish mental routines. The practice of mental conditioning will teach you how to be responsible by accepting the events, formulating responses and, therefore, perceiving the outcomes.

We are all capable of using this process to our benefit in life because we all have the ability to control our responses. We all have personal power. I refer to personal power as the ability to control one's focus, attitude and response to adversity — to choose one's own path in life.

THE HUMAN PAUSE

As was briefly mentioned, humans have the unique ability to become internally aware of their responses to external stimuli. The famous psychological study known as Pavlov's Dog Experiments represents groundbreaking research investigating conditioned and unconditioned responses to unconditioned and conditioned stimuli. Without going into all the details of classical (Pavlovian) conditioning, the takeaway relevant to mental conditioning is that when there is a stimulus, there is a response.

Humans are no different, except for our ability to become aware of our responses. This recognition of how we respond is vital to mental conditioning, because we can train ourselves to pause in between the stimulus and our response, again giving us personal power to choose our response. Once we are aware of our innate responses to certain stimuli, we have the power to control and change them. Most people are unaware of this unique human ability, and these are the people we say have poor self-control skills. **What they have is a non-trained pause to adversity and negative events**.

Start becoming aware of how you respond to certain stimuli. To gain awareness and challenge yourself to catch that pause between the event and your reaction, reflect on how you react to particular events. Those trained in discipline and response-ability face adverse stimuli with poise. They control their pause by taking a deep breath and responding in a manner conducive to the attainment of excellence. Developing control over that pause is what separates those who stay in control under pressure from those who crack.

Remember it this way: When the dog of adversity threatens with his dangerous jaws, control yourself with your human pause... and deep breath.

EMOTION CLOUDS REALITY

In the grind of our day, it is easy for your mind to become clouded by adversity. When you make a poor decision, or the apathy of your co-workers is at an all-time high, or you are just not operating to your full potential on that day, it is easy to let your emotions get the best of you. As an Athletic Administrator in pursuit of excellence, do not let your emotions cloud the reality of performance.

When you take emotion out of the picture, you tend to respond much more clearly. What does emotion do? Emotion clouds reality. In my work with athletic programs across the country, I see frustrated people fire off at students, coaches, fans and administrators. These people often approach minor and trivial situations as if they were life-or-death. Most times, after the outburst, there is regret that emotions overpowered sensible response-ability.

It is important to use the mental conditioning skills we've discussed in this book to maintain response-ability. This comes back to self-control – recognizing what is within your control and emotionally letting go of everything else. Rely on the "3P's" of peak performance (present, process, positive) as the conscience that reminds you of your ability to respond with excellence rather than emotion. Act out of routine and conditioned/trained response, not emotion.

RAVIZZA'S RULES OF CONTROL

The greatest coach I have ever had was my mentor at Cal State Fullerton, and he is an icon in the field of sport psychology. Dr. Ken Ravizza introduced me to his three rules of mental conditioning that I believe truly reflect the significance of response-ability as it relates to your role of Athletic Administrator.

I believe a peak performer in the leadership field must understand these rules of response-ability to give himself or herself the personal power to reach the summit of the Mountain of Excellence:

1. Before you can control your performance, you must be in control of yourself.

2. You have very little control of what goes on around you, but you have total control over how you choose to respond to it.

3. What you are aware of, you can control; what you are unaware of will control you.

Staying in control of yourself and recognizing what you can and can't control will allow you to mentally stay in a calm, centered and grounded place. Staying in control of yourself in the face of adversity is a skill set that must be repetitively practiced for its proper development; this will allow you to perform in pressure situations.

Understanding what you can and can't control, and choosing to focus on what you can control while letting go of what you can't, gives you the personal power to focus your time, energy and attention to achieve excellence.

The first step to self-control is having an awareness of what is going on around you and, more importantly, what is going on inside of you. Ultimately, the development of self-awareness will place the power of response-ability in your head and in your hands.

CAIN'S COACHING POINT:
Early on in this book, you learned the importance of forcing yourself to act differently than how you feel, shouldering that personal response-ability, and choosing to act how you would if you were confident and knew you were going to succeed regardless of the situation. How have you been doing at acting differently than how you feel? Where in your life can you act differently than how you feel, choosing your response, and giving yourself a better chance for success?

_____

_____

_____

PRAYER, PRIMAL, PERFECT?

In his book *Heads-Up Baseball*, Dr. Ken Ravizza points out that when baseball players get emotionally out of control, it usually manifests through their performance in three general ways. They become a Prayer, Primal, or Perfect player, all of which lead to a decreased level of performance. This example can be applied to your role of Athletic Administrator.

PRAYER: When you become a prayer administrator, you look to some higher power to help you perform in your tasks. You resign to faith in fate, and simply hope for the stars to align and present you with the desired result. You hope to get through the day without any problems vs. attacking your day with purpose and being on a mission.

PRIMAL: When you become a primal administrator, you resort back to the days of the caveman. You begin to act in a desperate and erratic manner that often leaves you out of control and emotionally frustrated, and the desired result remains elusive. You bear down and work harder, and are quick to criticize those around you. You think that the more effort and energy you give, the results will follow. You ignore your signal lights and try to push through while being in red lights for a long period of time. Anger sets in and resentment is soon to follow.

PERFECT: When you become the perfect administrator, you attempt to make everything perfect. You strive for perfection, and little mistakes prevent you from appreciating the beautiful imperfections that life can bring.   As we have discussed, performance oriented around perfection is a sure path to failure because nothing is perfect. Remember, performance is not about perfection; it is about progress.

As an administrator and, more importantly, a human being, you DO NOT want to fall under any of these three categories of Prayer, Primal or Perfect.

The defining question at the highest level is not who has the most talent, because talent is, for the most part, similar at the highest levels of performance. Instead, the question pertains to who is able to bring his/her mental talents to the table on a consistent basis and who has the ability to respond appropriately under the pressures of adversity.

As an Athletic Administrator, you want to move away from Prayer, Primal and Perfect and into PREPARED and PRESENT.   Mental preparation will assist you in the development of appropriate response-ability, giving yourself the best opportunity for performance excellence, one day at a time.

> "Have no fear of perfection. You'll never reach it."
>
> *Salvador Dali*
> *Artist*

TRAIN YOUR RESPONSE-ABILITY

Peak performance is contingent on personal response-ability in daily excellence. Excellence is largely about being accountable for your perspective and controlling your response to the adverse events that will inevitably occur during each day. Use the equation $E + R = O$ as a reminder that you control half of the equation and the outcome is a result of your perspective. When you train your response-ability, you place the power in your head.

All peak performers learn to take ownership of their past, command the present, and take charge of their future. Once you instill these values within your performance, you will gain the self-control necessary for performance excellence. Do not become a victim to events. Become a champion by developing the ability to respond appropriately to adversity

We all have the ability to respond appropriately, and the material throughout this book gives you the resources to do just that.

The Mountain of Excellence and the role of athletic administration call out to many performers, but the ones who reach the peak are those who have the response-ability to master the journey, stick to the process and overcome the adversity that makes this game so great. The Mountain of Excellence will put obstacles in your path and will humble you at times, just like in leadership and just like life.

CHAPTER #8 REVIEW

- If it is to be, it is up to me.

- Response-ability is taking ownership of your past, commanding your present and taking charge of your future.

- Event + Response = Outcome.

- When the dog of adversity threatens with his dangerous jaws, control yourself with your human pause... and breathe.

- Emotion clouds reality; learn to control it.

- Develop self-control by learning the three rules of response-ability.

- Prayer, Primal and Perfect are all undesirable states of performance mentality.

CHAPTER #9

RELAXATION, RECOVERY & MENTAL IMAGERY

> "The mind and body often cannot distinguish between real and imagined experiences. They are processed with the same psychoneuromuscular patterns."
>
> ***Brian Cain***

Most of the athletic administrators I work with have a hard time relaxing. This is often due to the competitive demands and mentality it takes to do things at a high level. As a peak performer, you spend a lot of time acting differently than how you feel and forcing yourself to keep on grinding, getting your exercise, getting out of bed early in the morning and working passionately to take your performance to the next level.

Another reason why many administrators have a hard time relaxing is that a large part of their lives is spent making themselves do the things they may not feel like doing but that are instrumental to peak performance in their field. This shows their necessary dedication and resolve to being the best; however, quality time devoted to relaxation and recovery is also necessary to maximize performance potential. ***The harder you work, the more important recovery is so that you can continue to work and perform at a high level.***

The ability to relax and turn off the competitive beast inside of you is essential to peak performers, and it is fundamental to developing peace of mind away from the office. ***When it comes to your ability to relax, you cannot make yourself relax, you must let yourself relax, and this is where athletic administrators often find the challenge.***

This performance state seems diametrically opposed to the intense focus demanded for performance excellence and is therefore difficult for most to achieve. When you are in a relaxed state, however, your heart rate is lower, your breathing becomes deeper, and this kick-starts the recovery/repair process for the body and brain. The more relaxed you are, the quicker you recover from the demands you place on yourself, and the quicker you can get back to performance and preparation at the highest level.

CAIN'S COACHING POINT:
Relaxation is a skill that must be practiced, and is a skill that can be developed with proper training, just like the fundamental physical skills practiced in athletics. Relaxation starts with controlling your breathing.

THE ABILITY TO RELAX IS INSIDE YOU

Everything you need to relax is already inside you. The world's most powerful tranquilizers already reside within your body. You have the ability to use these tranquilizers to put yourself to sleep at night, and you can train yourself to tap into one of the most powerful resources of your body and mind throughout the day, whenever you experience stress, pressure and anxiety.

Administrators have reported to me that, if they could relax, it would help their daily performance. Knowing they need to relax is not the problem; the problem is that they often do not know how, because they have never been taught the simple strategy for relaxation.

Let's face it. When a colleague or friend says to you, "Hey, just relax!" (which I heard my entire career as an athlete,) it does nothing to help you. In reality, it often makes you tenser, because now you know that your colleague or friend has picked up on the fact that you are stressed out and full of anxiety. Instead of telling someone to relax, ask them to take a good deep breath. Taking a deep breath is the single most valuable and effective exercise one must learn to use in order to enter a more relaxed and present state.

THE CALMING OF CAIN

When I was a college baseball player at the University of Vermont, the part of my game that held me back the most was my inability to relax and keep my mind productively focused in the present moment, one pitch at a time. My mind would get moving so fast that I could not keep it on the one thought that mattered, the execution of that particular pitch. My mind would be thinking about how this was my opportunity to make up for my previous mistakes; to finally show my coaches, teammates, and myself that I was good; that I was worthy of the scholarship or the playing time I had been given; and that, if I could perform at the level of my expectations, I could be one of the best.

As you can tell, the gears would begin to move faster and faster until I could hardly breathe; and before I knew it, I was ready to come out of the game before it even started.

My senior year of college I took a stress management class with the University of Vermont gymnastics coach Gary Bruning. Luckily for me, it was more of an applied stress management class than a theory-based class. He taught the class *how* to mentally and physically relax instead of teaching textbook theories of stress management and the physiological effects of stress that I had experienced. I was very aware of the fact that I did not know how to relax, so I embraced the opportunity for self-improvement as Coach Bruning taught us all how to relax.

He had us lie down on the floor and talked us through a series of deep-breathing exercises. I put my hand on my stomach and focused intently on breathing in through my nostrils and out through my mouth, while feeling my stomach rise with the inhalation and lower with the exhalation of each breath. After about fifteen minutes of feeling weird just lying there and feeling like I should be doing something else, with my mind racing 100MPH, I finally experienced my mind slowing down and my body and mind relaxing.

I was 22 years old, a senior in college, and I can still vividly remember experiencing the ability to relax for the first time in my life. It was a revolutionary mind-body experience, and utterly unfamiliar to me. I could slow my mind down and focus into the present through my newfound ability to relax. I could now also speed up my recovery process simply by focusing on my breathing. To this day, I am grateful that I enrolled in that course and for Coach Bruning's applied method of teaching.

MAXIMIZING OXYGEN IN THE OCTAGON

As a mental conditioning coach, nowhere have I seen relaxation and deep breathing serve a more vital function for performance excellence than in the Ultimate Fighting Championship. The world's most combative, most competitive sport of mixed martial arts is a ballet of violence by nature. Some people may find it too brutal for their liking, but this cannot discredit the fearless mentality it takes to step inside of the Octagon and go to battle. We can learn a lot from what happens mentally inside the Octagon that can assist peak performance in administration and leadership. In my work with college and high school athletic programs, I teach a lot of the very same mental skills that I train the best MMA fighters on the planet, such as Georges St. Pierre and Vitor Belfort, to have in their mental game arsenal.

In mixed martial arts, it is often the fighter who can relax first and move the fight into his specialty who wins. While the fighters work on bringing the fight to them, some of the greatest coaches in the game can be heard reinforcing the importance of breathing to help their fighter athletes relax. As a coach, the verbal cue for an athlete to take a breath is a reminder of what the athlete must do to calm down and perform at a more relaxed state. The more an athlete practices his breathing exercises to relax and quiet his mind outside of the Octagon, the more the brain and body know how to respond when he takes the deep breath inside the Octagon. As with everything in peak performance, you must learn to be in control of yourself physically and mentally before you can control your performance, and the most crucial practice to gain self-control is deep breathing.

I see the MMA fighter taking a deep breath in his corner between rounds the same as an Athletic Administrator taking a deep breath between classes/meetings and applying these principles to train their coaches how to apply this to their teams during intense game situations.

RELAXED INTENSITY

The best Athletic Administrators perform with a relaxed intensity. These leaders become so immersed in their present-moment focus of execution that they are calm and poised, yet fully engaged and energized. Their competitive concentration appears unbreakable. Nothing can distract them; no adversity fazes them. They are "locked in" and it is as if they are operating on another level. Well, they ARE on another level; this is performance excellence! Now it's time for you to join them on that level.

CAIN'S COACHING POINT:
This peak performance state of excellence is different than "The Zone." Personally, I believe "The Zone" to be a place of quiet mind and quiet body where you are performing at your best.

I think "The Zone" is a place that we waste too much time talking about and trying to get to. I do not believe you can recreate "The Zone," but I do believe that you can get much closer to the state of peak performance through mental conditioning in distraction control, battling and dealing with adversity, acting differently than you feel, and competing all out, every day. I invest my time in coaching how to mentally persevere and have good bad days; I do not focus on getting into "The Zone." Remember, you cannot always control how you feel, but you can choose how you act. Think of confidence as an ACTION more than a feeling.

RELAXATION IS A SKILL ANYONE CAN DEVELOP

As with all mental conditioning techniques, relaxation is a skill that can be learned and developed through training. Relaxation is a skill that requires mastering everything previously covered in this book. The ability to relax is founded upon a present-moment focus on the process of what you can control, along with a perspective of positivity that has been practiced over and over so that it has become routine.

I want you to think of the ability to relax as a skill, just like the physical skills you would use in any sport. If you can dribble, shoot and catch a basketball, your ability to execute that skill is because you have trained yourself to perform it. You have practiced and you have conditioned that skill, investing time and effort into improving it. I want you to do the same for the mental conditioning skill of relaxation.

THE 5-4-3-2-1 RELAXATION/FOCUS EXERCISE

I want to walk you through a relaxation and focus exercise called the 5-4-3-2-1 exercise. By understanding how to breathe properly and practicing the process of a 5-4-3-2-1 relaxation technique until it becomes a routine relaxation procedure, you give yourself the best opportunity to relax under pressure and perform at your best.

CAIN'S COACHING POINT:
I have created a series of relaxation training audios, including the 5-4-3-2-1 audio, that you can listen to as part of my Monday Message Series at <u>www.BrianCain.com/ Monday</u> (search for Daily Mental Practice).

TWO TYPES OF BREATHING

There are two types of breathing: diaphragmatic breathing and shoulder breathing. Diaphragmatic breathing is deep breathing, using your diaphragm and abdominal muscles. To identify this type of breathing, place your hand on your stomach and feel your abdominal muscles expand as you inhale and contract as you exhale. During this deep breathing, air entirely fills your lungs and maximizes oxygen intake. Shoulder breathing, on the other hand, only reaches the top of your lungs. Often referred to as shallow breathing, shoulder breathing is often the result of a performer's inability to relax, resulting in tight muscles that exacerbate this tight breathing. As an administrator in a high-stress field, you must learn the proper method of deep breathing.

It is also important to know where to breathe. For proper relaxation, one should inhale through the nose, because the nose acts as a natural air filter, and exhale out your mouth, giving you a more forceful release. As you inhale, I want you to perform a count of 8; then as you exhale, perform a count of 10, making your exhalation a little bit longer than your inhalation.

SCRIPT FOR THE 5-4-3-2-1 RELAXATION SESSION

This is a script that you can have read to you or you can read to your teams to help them practice and develop the skill of relaxation. You will want to read it slowly and in a monotone voice, or you can simply play the audio for them that is available on my website above.

The first thing you want to do is put yourself in a quiet, comfortable environment. Sit up straight in your chair, hands in your lap or on the desk in front of you, feet flat on the floor. Please look at a spot on the wall in front of you, and focus on that spot.

Now, let your eyes gently close as you inhale, breathing deeply through your nose. As you inhale, your shoulders and chest should not move. Focus on breathing steadily and deeply through the nose, pushing out all your abdominal muscles as your diaphragm expands and air fills the bottom of your lungs. Now, exhale through your mouth, as your abdominal muscles and diaphragm contract and the air exits your lungs.

As you continue to focus on your breathing, having a count of 8 on the inhalation and 10 on the exhalation, realize that everything you need to relax is already inside you. The world's most powerful tranquilizers lay within. The ability to relax is a skill that needs to be developed, and you are doing that now. You need to train to relax just like you do for the skills required to be the best leader possible.

Answer the following three questions as you continue to focus on your breathing. Answer these questions in your mind and notice how the answers just pop into your head:

1. What is 3 x 3?

2. What is your middle name?

3. What street did you grow up on?

Notice how easily and effortlessly the answers popped into your mind. The ability to relax is a skill that can be trained, developed and called upon just as easily as answering those three questions.

We will now go through a short body scan, in which you are to focus your awareness into the body parts that are mentioned.

When you hear the number 5, let your toes, the balls of your feet, arches, heels, your ankles, your Achilles tendon, your calves and your shins release, relax and let go.

When you hear the number 4, let your knees, your quads, your hamstrings, your hips, your whole lower body release, relax and let go, sinking further and further into the chair that you are sitting on.

When you hear the number 3, let your lower back, your mid back, your upper back, your abs, your obliques, your ribs, your pectorals and your whole torso release, relax and let go.

What you will find is that, the more relaxed you become, the better you might feel; and the better you feel, the more relaxed you will want to become.

When you hear the number 2, relax your traps, your shoulders, your biceps, your triceps, your forearms, your hands and your fingers — just release, relax and let go.

When you hear the number 1, relax the back of your neck, the back of your head, the top of your head, your forehead, your eyes, your cheeks and your jaw; let your lips gently part and your tongue hang in your mouth as a complete and total body of relaxation takes over.

What you will realize is that the more relaxed you become, the better you will feel; and the better you feel, the more relaxed you will want to become.

Take another deep breath.

Now, gently open your eyes and bring yourself back to this moment, right here, right now.

This concludes the 5-4-3-2-1 relaxation session.

Once you have this audio recording readily available to you, you should do this once a day.

CONTROL THE ENVIRONMENT

In order to properly condition your relaxation, you must begin training in a controlled environment. Initial relaxation training should occur in a quiet and controlled environment where you can relax in peace. This enables you to focus on the process of relaxation in that moment, ignoring all other stimuli and emptying the mind of unnecessary thoughts.

After you have practiced in this controlled and quiet environment for a few weeks, slowly integrate adversity to simulate a more chaotic or competitive environment similar to an athletic event.

Introduce crowd noise or music in the background of your controlled setting, and practice your relaxation response to this adversity by focusing on your breathing. Audio simulates adversities that will become distractions if you let them get into your head. Do not let them get in your head; instead, focus on the next breath. Use your relaxed state of mind to push distractions far away by locking into what you want to focus on, going one breath at a time.

Once you have trained your ability to relax under simulated adversity in a controlled environment, the next step is to perform your relaxation technique in performance practices, then in pressure-packed scenarios. During these preparation sessions, you will further practice the execution of your relaxation techniques, and eventually this will translate to an execution and peak performance during your day.

CONTROL YOURSELF

As I am sure you have gathered by now, breathing is the foundation for relaxation. Simultaneously, breathing is the basis for emotional state management, a.k.a. self-control. Relaxation conditions self-control by teaching you how to become grounded within the self. When you focus on your breathing, your mind and body become one in the present moment. The relaxation process is proven to reduce stress levels and alleviate anxiety, giving you control of your emotional state. Good breathing makes all the difference in self-control, and thus in the achievement of performance excellence.

CONDITIONING THE RELAXATION RESPONSE

If you have never trained your breathing and you try to relax by taking a deep breath in a pressure situation, the body and the brain will not be conditioned to respond by gaining control of yourself. If you condition yourself to relax through the routine practice of deep breathing, first in the quiet, controlled environment and then in more disruptive scenarios, by the time you call upon it in a highly stressful situation, it will be a skill you have developed and it will be there when you need it.

When you practice the 5-4-3-2-1 technique, you will feel more connected to the present moment, more relaxed and more in control of yourself. The more you train with the 5-4-3-2-1 technique, the more you focus on your breathing; and the more you do your relaxation training, the more this relaxation preparation is going to help in practices and games. The goal is for this technique to become so routine that, when you take a deep breath to help you relax, your body will be conditioned to respond by relaxing and getting you into a place of self-control. When this occurs, you will know you have a properly conditioned relaxation response.

RELAXATION IN THE RECOVERY PROCESS

For Athletic Administrators to take their daily performance to the next level, they must constantly put their bodies and minds in uncomfortable and stressful situations where they are challenged to adapt and evolve. To consistently bring a high level of energy and effort to these situations, administrators must be able to recover outside of their competitive arena.

Relaxation is a tremendous facilitator of recovery. The more relaxed you are, the greater the recovery process, thus assisting your physical and mental regeneration so that you can continue to compete and train at your highest level.

> "Tension is who you think you should be. Relaxation is who you are."
>
> ***Chinese Proverb***

RECOVERY PROCESS

As you are probably well aware, there is a physical recovery process after physical performance in which the body goes to work repairing the damage done to muscle tissue. After an exercise session, which should be part of your daily routine, it is this physical recovery process that builds the muscle you desire for daily performance and increase in productivity. Not surprisingly, there is a mental recovery process of releasing stress and anxiety that is equally important. In the process, these two forms of recovery often converge, blending similar practices and exercises to maximize both forms of recovery. All administrators and leaders should be aware of the significance of recovery on performance, and understand that both your physical and mental recoveries are enhanced when in a relaxed state.

CAIN'S GAME PLAN:
If you were to grade your ability to relax on a 1-10 scale, with 10 being the best, you would give yourself a grade of ?

1 2 3 4 5 6 7 8 9 10

To help yourself move one number closer to 10, you will do the following:

_____

_____

THE MAGIC 20-MINUTE WINDOW OF RECOVERY

Dr. Declan Connolly is a world-renowned exercise physiologist, sports nutritionist, and strength and conditioning coach. He is a professor at the University of Vermont, and a consultant to the New York Rangers among other professional teams and Olympic organizations. He also was my college undergraduate advisor at the University of Vermont, and remains to this day a close personal friend and mentor on the physiological aspects of performance. Dr. Connolly speaks of the importance of the sports nutrition magic 20-minute window.

The magic 20-minute window of sports nutrition indicates that you want to have food in your system, whether it is a protein shake, a peanut butter and jelly sandwich or even a Snickers bar, within the 20-minute period after finishing a workout, to help speed up the recovery process.

The recovery benefits of getting food into your system within 20 minutes after the completion of a workout will be greater than if you had steak and potatoes 45 minutes to 1 hour after a workout. Physically and mentally, the recovery process is kick-started when you can get these much-needed proteins, carbohydrates and fats into your system within that window. Developing the discipline to bring food with you for post-performance a snack is important to enhance your recovery process. It is equally important that you force yourself to act on your knowledge of recovery, because many report they do not feel like eating after performance. If you let your feelings dictate your actions, you lose in leadership and in life.

CAIN'S COACHING POINT:
Keep a refrigerator in your office that is packed with water and nutrient-rich foods. Many administrators skip meals because they "have too much to do." Failure to fuel your body will result in diminished energy levels and lowered productivity levels. For you to be the best you need to be at your best, which means feeding your machine.

DISCIPLINE IS THE KEY TO RECOVERY

The hardest part about eating inside of the magic 20-minute window after completing a workout is having the discipline to bring food with you to the gym or the office. Establishing a disciplined routine of bringing yourself a simple peanut butter and jelly sandwich on wheat bread, a piece of fruit or a protein shake, and getting that food into your system within that 20-minute window, will dramatically speed up your recovery process.

ONE-THIRD OF YOUR LIFE – INVEST IN A BED

If you knew you were going to spend one-third of your life performing a sport, you would want to gather all the information you could, and educate yourself on how to achieve performance excellence in that sport. If you knew you were going to work a specific job for one-third of your life, I'll bet you would also want to become as knowledgeable and proficient as possible to achieve job performance excellence. So why would sleep, which you will do for approximately one-third of your life, be any different? Unfortunately, you probably know very little about what goes on physiologically when you sleep, so let's get you started with some general knowledge about the importance of sleep for your recovery. It is the #1 most important factor and place that you can get a competitive advantage.

POWER SLEEP

Dr. James Maas is a professor at Cornell University, and one of the world's leading authorities and experts on sleep. In his books *Power Sleep* and *Sleep to Win*, he breaks down the information you need to know about sleeping, and how much you need it to perform at your peak. As a scholar, he has addressed the physiological benefits of sleep and the issue of severe sleep deprivation that plagues most college and high school athletes, resulting in performances that represent about 80% of their potential. If you don't like to read, check him out on YouTube. This might be the missing link to your performance. I am getting sleepy as I type this... ☺

An individual is considered to be sleep-deprived if he or she sleeps four hours or less per night, while eight hours constitutes normal sleep. The National Sleep Foundation's sleep guidelines recommend seven to nine hours for the average adult. Dr. Maas suggests in *Power Sleep* that you get 9 hours and 15 minutes of sleep a night so that you will receive your five REM (Rapid Eye Movement) cycles, thus maximizing the physiological benefits of your recovery time in sleep. One night of missed sleep will probably do little harm, but the cumulative effect of poor sleep will have a negative impact on your performance.

Sleep is an active physiological process, one in which your body is busy carrying out vital activities while you are unconscious. While asleep, your body alternates between two forms of sleep: rapid eye movement (REM) and non-REM sleep. This cycle repeats several times throughout the night. The stage of REM sleep provides the brain with the energy to support it during waking hours and is necessary for restoring the mind to function at a level of peak performance. These physiological processes are significant for your psyche, because mental conditioning is most effective when an individual's psychological state is in sync with an optimum physiological state.

10 TIPS FOR SOUND SLEEPING

1. **Relax Before Retiring** – Take some time for a pre-sleep ritual to break the connection between stress and bedtime. Try listening to the 5-4-3-2-1 relaxation session, listening to relaxation music, doing some light stretching or taking a hot shower.

2. **Watch the Caffeine** – Caffeine is the stimulant present in coffee (100-200 mg), soda (50-75 mg), tea (50-75 mg) and various over-the-counter medications. Caffeine should not be consumed for at least four to six hours before bedtime.

3. **Watch the Alcohol** – Although alcohol is a depressant and may help you fall asleep, the subsequent metabolism that clears it from your body while you are sleeping causes a withdrawal syndrome. This withdrawal causes awakenings and is often associated with nightmares and sweats. To help reduce some of these effects, try drinking one glass of water for every alcoholic beverage consumed. And stop all liquid consumption at least two hours before bedtime so that you are not waking up in the middle of the night to urinate.

4. **Exercise at the Right Time** – Regular exercise relieves stress and encourages good sleep. However, if a little exercise really gets your blood pumping, it would be wise to avoid working out in the evening or just before bedtime.

5. **Cut Down on Noise, Light, and Extreme Temperatures** – Try earplugs, a night-light, an eye mask or a drape clip. The best temperature for sleep is 65-69 degrees.

6. **Eat Right and Sleep Tight** – Avoid eating a large meal just before bedtime or going to bed hungry. It is about balance. Also, whenever possible, opt for foods that promote sleep, such as milk, tuna, halibut, artichokes, oats, asparagus, potatoes and bananas.

7. **Understanding Jet Lag** – Before you cross time zones, try waking up later or earlier to help your body adjust to the time difference. It takes approximately one day for each hour you fly to adjust to a new time zone. Many people are affected more severely by West to East travel than East to West. Anticipate that it may take a few days for your body to catch up, and you can speed up that process by easing yourself into the new time zone schedule before you leave.

8. **Respect the Purpose of the Bed** – Avoid TV, eating and emotional discussions while in bed. The mind and body associate bedtime activities with being in bed. Do not let a bad habit keep you awake.

9. **Nap Smart** – A power nap early in the afternoon can really refresh you. Make it brief – no more than 20 minutes. Sleep too much and you may spend the night staring at the ceiling.

10. **Pet Sleepers** – Does your pet sleep with you? This, too, may cause arousals from either allergies or their movements in the bed. Thus, Yotie and Cypress (my two French Bulldogs) may be better off on the floor than on the sheets.

Be sure to invest in the best mattress you can afford. How you spend the 1/3 of your life you invest in bed will determine how you are able to invest the other 2/3 of your life out of bed. Invest in yourself. Invest in your rest and recovery. Invest in the best mattress you can buy.

OLYMPIC SLEEP TRICKS

The USA Olympic organization will often go into the Olympic Village ahead of the games and put in extended-length beds and blackout curtains in the rooms of all its athletes. This is because the organization recognizes how important sleep is to its athletes' peak performance. The USOC wants to give our athletes the best opportunity to bring home the gold and so it invests wisely in sleep.

As an adult, sleep can often be at a minimum. Throw a couple of kids in the mix who enjoy burning the midnight oil, and you have got a recipe for poor sleep. The quality of your sleep has become more important than ever, as well as finding opportunities to get caught back up. On the nights when there is nothing happening at school or with school to occupy your time, go to bed early and take advantage of the moment. Be on the same page with your spouse on those early bed nights and use them as an opportunity to read and relax; turn off the meaningless game on TV and invest in your own health. You will not regret getting those extra couple of hours, but you most definitely will regret losing the extra hours for something mindless.

CAIN'S EXPENSIVE EXPERIENCE ON RECOVERY

When I was Athletic Administrator in my early 20s, I always thought I was capable of more than was requested of me, and that the longer and harder I worked, the better I would become. I was constantly working long hours and doing more than was expected. I let my sleep numbers slip and my exercise programming went out the window. My nutrition plan was whatever was in front of my face, and the level of health that I strived for had not become a priority. What I failed to realize was the significant difference between working harder versus working smarter, and that the more I worked, the more I needed to recover and refocus my efforts.

Much like my college days, I never had a plan for recovery or for a great sleep routine, and I probably slept around 4-6 hours a night in college. When I was working as an Athletic Administrator, many nights went well past midnight. I was the guy who would pull all-nighters, thinking I could operate, so jacked up on caffeine that I would crash in the middle of it, be thinking too fast and be jumpy, or I would walk in and simply not recall any of the goals for my day because I was so tired. When great friend and mentor Jason Spector called me out on my routines and took notice of my 245-

pound body, I knew that I had to change.

I got locked in on my nutrition and the plan I put in place to know my numbers of proteins, carbohydrates, and fats to hit each day. When I combined that with an exercise routine and improved sleep habits, I dropped 50 pounds to 195 and am in the best shape of my life. I realized quickly that by letting myself go in favor of others and my job was not selfless – it was selfish. For me to be at my best for others, I needed to be at my best for myself first. The increase in energy and functionality of my physical self has allowed me to maintain the full schedule and active lifestyle. If you are a casualty of poor recovery and activity habits, take a hard look at yourself and what it's doing to your daily performance. It's never too late to change.

YOGA AS A MENTAL CONDITIONING EXERCISE

Again, it was my course with Coach Bruning that turned my life and recovery routines in a productive and progressive direction. Coach Bruning taught yoga to the class as a source of both physiological and psychological relaxation. Practicing and understanding the benefits of yoga have really helped me become more familiar with my body and manage my emotional state. During that course, I improved my flexibility and learned how to breathe and find my center of balance, both physically and mentally.

Ironically, before the 2013-2014 NFL season, there was a fantastic article on ESPN.com about the Seattle Seahawks and how they used yoga as a part of their pre-practice routine to gain better control of their breath and their physical/mental/emotional self. Many professional sports teams have hired yoga instructors for their players as well. In one more strike of irony, my wife Erin also happens to be a yoga instructor, and the sessions invested in her studio have allowed me to continue to develop my focus, balance and intentional breathing.

RE-CENTER YOURSELF

Relaxation and recovery are both critical elements within a peak performer's mental conditioning program. Training your relaxation response through deep breathing will help you stay locked into the present moment, think more clearly, and perform more fluidly during your day. Relaxation outside of your arena will help you speed up the recovery process, enabling you to return and perform harder, longer and smarter as you take your administrative performance to the next level.

Throughout life, it is important to use these relaxation and recovery practices to constantly re-center yourself, because internal balance leads to the performance consistency necessary for all peak performers. As you climb the Mountain of Excellence, remember to pause, take a deep breath and re-center yourself. This will keep you climbing at your most productive pace and living this life one moment at a time.

MENTAL IMAGERY

At this moment, imagine performing your end-of-the-day routine, walking around the facilities to check on the practices that are taking place. You begin in the gym to see the volleyball coach taking the players through a drill, with the players going through their pre-serve routines and final thoughts. The coaches are intentional with their commands and then the most impressive display of serving takes place in front of your eyes. When a great serve is made, the girls quickly refocus onto the next rep. When a bad serve is made, the girls breathe, give a physical release, and refocus while the coaches yell, "So what, next serve!"

You move outside to find your cross country coaches talking to the athletes about tomorrow's upcoming race. The coaches break the race into segments and focus on competing during each segment, with performance indicators for each athlete on where they should be at that specific time in the race. The coach finishes the talk with the following statement: "It's not about running to beat a person or to a specific place. That is outside of your control. It's running to beat the course and to attack each of the 4 segments in the race to the best of your ability. The result will take care of itself." This is music to your ears.

The rounds will be finished up at the practice football field. You observe the coaches hollering, "Flush it! Do not let one play affect the next. You have 35 seconds to refocus before the next play happens. Get your mind right and be where your feet are." Players are all actively engaged in practice with no standing around. The players who are standing behind are getting practice on the appropriate steps to take out of their stance that are crucial to the installation process of the new play action boot series. After a rep is completed, each player practices his own refocus routine before getting back to the line where the preparation process repeats.

You walk away from the walk-through evaluations and end-of-the-day routine proud as ever. The coaching staff and athletes are responding well to the Championship Culture and mental game. You beam as you call your spouse on the drive home to talk about what you witnessed. It is a moment unlike any other!

As you drive home in reflection over the manifestation of your work, a feeling of accomplishment washes over you. A difference is being made here! This is it. In this moment, you have reached the mountaintop.

You walk as a champion. With the utmost satisfaction, you know you have given your best when you needed it the most, and that your performance has been simply superior. Your PRIDE – Personal Responsibility In Daily Excellence, your making all of your todays count, and not counting them over all those years of training – has culminated in this. All of the hard work and dedication to your craft has been rewarded. You are the epitome of peak performance in athletic administration.

This imaginary scenario is your introduction to mental imagery. Now, let's make that vision a reality.

CAIN'S COACHING POINT:
Everything happens twice: First in your mind, then in reality. Mental imagery is one of the most well-researched mental skills that is NOT being used on a consistent basis. That means mental imagery is a place where you can get a competitive advantage through increased preparation and the resulting confidence.

HEAD REHEARSAL

One of the most underutilized mental conditioning skills is mental imagery. Mental imagery, often referred to as visualization, is the process of creating mental experiences that resemble actual physical experiences, similar to watching a highlight video of your best performance in your mind.

This process is similar to the stimulation of the imagination when you read an excerpt in second-person narrative, such as the introduction to this chapter. The difference is that the script is not on a piece of paper in front of you, it is all in your head.

In mental conditioning, mental imagery is used to enhance performance preparation and build confidence. It is a technique employed to exercise the mind by mentally creating the environment of performance competition, and mentally performing the leadership tasks required in your mind. Mentally, you rehearse how you want to feel and how you want to perform, imagining the integration of your physical conditioning and your mental conditioning within your mind to see your best performance before you step out into your arena to do battle.

THE MIND-BODY CONNECTION

Mental imagery has the potential to make a HUGE impact in your daily performance. Whether you vividly imagine or you physically execute your performance, the brain processes those two experiences with similar psychoneuromuscular pathways. Made simple, that means you are hard-wiring your brain and body for peak performance.

Mental imagery is creating neural patterns in your brain in the same manner as the performance of a physical action. Essentially, if you are lying in bed at night and you practice mental imagery, you are imprinting the blueprint of your performance in your mind, further embedding those pathways and enhancing your capacity to achieve what it is you see in your mind when you step onto the field.

CAIN'S COACHING POINT:
Before you get carried away, however, let's get one thing

clear: Mental imagery is not a substitute for physical preparation. This is not some shortcut or fast track to peak performance. Putting in the physical time is necessary. The mental conditioning technique of mental imagery enhances your physical abilities by deepening those psychoneuromuscular pathways in your brain. Mental imagery is utilized to maximize the efficiency and effectiveness of your physical preparation. You still must be a "Do-er".

YOU ARE "THE ARCHITECT" OF YOUR VISION

In order to emphasize how an individual practices mental imagery, I've drawn a parallel to a concept from the Warner Brothers blockbuster movie *Inception*. In the film, a complex plot revolves around dreams and characters' movements in and out of the dream world. There are particular characters in the movie called "architects," who build infinitely detailed dream worlds that mirror reality. This movie is one of the ultimate mind-benders in cinema, and if you haven't seen it, I apologize for using this particular analogy. However, this concept of "architects" is exactly what you want to emulate in your process of mental imagery.

When you perform the mental conditioning technique of mental imagery, you create a mental world. You construct in your mind a psychological replica of your arena (office, locker room, stadium, classroom, etc.), and place yourself within that arena. When you perform mental imagery, you want to build in the sense of sight, the sense of sound, and the sense of touch. You want to mentally experience the appearance of where you will be, what you will be doing, and the situation that exists. The more details you construct as the architect of the video in your mind, the greater you enhance the effectiveness of the mental imagery experience.

PHYSIOLOGICAL BENEFITS FROM PSYCHOLOGICAL STIMULUS

If you are still a little skeptical about mental imagery, then I want to give you a little taste of the mind-body connection. I want you to experience the physiological response to the psychological stimulus of mental imagery. Before telling you to just go off and practice mental imagery, I will walk you through a scenario.

Whenever you perform mental imagery, recall and practice the techniques of relaxation to help you focus more clearly on the mental imagery process.

So sit back and focus on your breathing. Go through the process of relaxation and practice your deep breathing as you read the passage below, or have someone read it to you.

I am going to walk you through a scenario where you go into your kitchen, reach into your refrigerator, pull out a lemon, cut lemon wedges, and take a bite out of one of those lemon wedges. Read slowly and imagine the scenario in all its detail. Practice utilizing all your senses in this passage, because you want to make this scenario feel as real as possible in your mind.

THE LEMON EXPERIMENT

Start by taking 3 good breaths using an 8-count on your inhalation and a 10-count on your exhalation. Breathe in nice and deep through your nose and release out through your mouth.

Now, imagine walking into your kitchen at home. Feel what the floor feels like on your bare feet.

You are now standing in front of your refrigerator. See the refrigerator in front of you in all its detail. Now, extend your hand outward, reaching for the refrigerator door, and clasp the door handle.

As you open that refrigerator door, notice a nice big, bright yellow lemon on the top shelf.

Reach for it and grab it. As you hold it in the palm of your hand, see the skin and feel the coolness and texture of that lemon as you feel its weight in your hand.

Put that lemon on the counter, take a knife lying there, and use it to cut the lemon in half the long way. See the juice and the body of that lemon as the knife slices through. Smell the slightly sour scent released into the air. Take half of the cut lemon and cut it again, so that you have two equal wedges. See and feel the sting of the lemon juice on your wet fingertips. Breathe in that lemon scent swelling in the air.

Now gently place your fingers, wet with lemon juice, on either side of a lemon wedge and lift it off the counter. Bring it up to your mouth and close your lips around the wedge before sinking your teeth along the lemon rind and squeezing the lemon juice into your mouth. Feel the lemon juice squirt onto the back of your tongue and the back of your mouth. Feel that sensation at the back of your teeth as you press your tongue against them to get all the lemon juice.

Remove the lemon and place the deflated wedge back on the counter.

A TASTE OF THE IMAGE

Did you have a bit of a puckering sensation? Did your mouth salivate at the thought of the lemon taste? Could you smell that lemon or feel the sour juice sting your taste buds? Just thinking about the process of eating lemon made me salivate while I wrote this passage.

If you did receive any of those sensations as you read the passage, then you have now consciously experienced a physiological response (the body responding) to a psychological stimulus. This is a simple firsthand experience that emphasizes the shared psychoneuromuscular pathways of the brain and body. Remember this experience and try to simulate the realness of eating the lemon in your mental imagery when you visualize yourself being at your best in every area of your life.

If you did not experience a physiological response, then you probably read the passage too fast and didn't immerse yourself in this psychological scenario... or maybe you just did not eat enough lemons as a kid! But seriously, in order to properly utilize mental imagery, you MUST use the techniques of relaxation that you have learned. You must become absolutely immersed in the present mental rehearsal you are performing, releasing all mental bricks and deflecting all distractions.

PRACTICING ADVERSITY

A great way to utilize the benefits of mental imagery is to create a list of situations in your job that make you uncomfortable and represent some form of adversity. Once you have made this list, use it as a checklist and use mental imagery to perform under each adverse scenario, executing exactly the way you want to in performance. This is similar to the favorite physical practice of children acting out a last-second scenario, where their team is down one and they hit the game-winning shot as they count down 5, 4, 3, 2, 1! Both practices deal with adverse situations and both imagine a desired outcome.

IMAGINE YOUR EXCELLENCE

Mental imagery is one of the most basic and fundamental of all mental conditioning strategies; however, it is widely underused. Remember that actions speak louder than words. You now have a greater understanding of the power of mental imagery; you just need to DO mental imagery in order to increase your performance preparation and confidence. Believe BIG and what you want, for **you will never outperform your own self-image.**

4 STEPS OF MENTAL IMAGERY

Doing mental imagery is as easy as closing your eyes and watching your human highlight reel in your mind. It does not need to get more complex than that. When I train administrators and coaches to take themselves and their teams through mental imagery the night before games, I outline four steps so that they have a rhythm and routine to follow:

1. **Relaxation** – Take them through the 5-4-3-2-1 technique.

2. **Confidence Conditioning** – Take them through the positive affirmations you want them to hear and that you want to embed into

their mental game. Say each statement three times with enough time between statements so the players can repeat them to themselves.

3. **Mental Recall** – Have the players recall and revisit the best days of their career. They replay those big moments in their minds as if the past were happening now.

4. **Mental Rehearsal** – Have the players go forward to their next performance and visualize how exactly they want to perform. You can talk them through very specific situations that you have been preparing for.

CHAPTER #9 REVIEW

- We all possess the ability to relax.

- Aim to perform with a relaxed intensity.

- Relaxation is the secret to results under pressure.

- Relaxation is a skill one must develop like any other physical skill.

- Diaphragmatic breathing is superior to shoulder breathing.

- Practice the 5-4-3-2-1 technique to build a relaxation response.

- Begin training your relaxation response in a controlled environment and progress under simulated adversity.

- Emotional state management is all about self-control and breathing.

- Relaxation is instrumental to recovery process.

- Invest in your sleep – it is the most important part of the recovery process.

- Relaxation before bed facilitates productive sleep, benefiting physiological and psychological recovery.

- Mental conditioning is most effective when an individual's psychological state is reflective of an optimum physiological state.

- Internal balance leads to the performance consistency necessary for all peak performers.

- You cannot make yourself relax; you must *let* yourself relax.

- Mental imagery is the process of creating mental experiences that resemble physical experience.

- Mental performance creates physiological neural patterns in your brain in the same manner as the performance of physical action.

- As a mental architect, you want to build experiences using all the senses within your mental performance.

- Mental imagery enhances psychoneuromuscular pathways to assist physical rehabilitation.

- Practice mental performance before beginning physical competition.

- Watching videos of your best performances benefits your mental imagery by giving you a positive visual.

- Practice handling adversity in mental imagery as you do during preparation.

CHAPTER #10

INSPIRATION & MOTIVATION

> "A man can be as great as he wants to be. If you believe in yourself and have the courage, the determination, the dedication, the competitive drive and if you are willing to sacrifice the little things in life and pay the price for the things that are worthwhile, it can be done.
>
> **Vince Lombardi**
> **NFL Hall of Fame Coach**
> **Super Bowl Champion**

I was in Dallas, Texas, at a fair and on a stage was a big, muscular strongman performing some amazing feats of strength. He was ripping phone books in half and bending crowbars with his hands to the thunderous applause of his audience.

In one of his acts, he pulled out a lemon and squeezed all the juice out of that lemon and said: "Ladies and gentlemen, I am a strongman. I've squeezed all the juice out of this lemon. I will give $1,000 to anyone who can come up and extract one more drop."

In response, two giant Dallas Cowboy-like guys went on stage to give it a try. The first guy grabbed the lemon and gave it a good, hard squeeze. No drop! The crowd laughed in amusement as he stepped back to let his friend give the lemon a squeeze. The crowd went silent and watched the second guy give the lemon a squeeze, contorting his face in grimaced concentration. He suddenly released his grip with a gasp for air, but still not one drop of lemon juice.

The crowd laughed and applauded as the two men exited the stage. The strongman was left on stage holding his arms in the air with the lemon in his hand when he saw an old lady, who looked to be in her seventies, walking up the stairs onto the stage.

The strongman said: "Ma'am, for the sake of time, can we move on? You are not going to squeeze any juice out of the lemon. I mean, c'mon. The guys who just tried couldn't do it, and they looked like professional football players."

"Sir, just give me a chance," the old lady said politely.

"Okay. Here you go. One chance," said the strongman, who handed her the lemon as the crowd cheered in support.

The old lady took the lemon within her hands and began to squeeze. Her face became contorted. Her jaw set. Her veins began popping out of her forehead. Her glasses fell off her face. Her entire body shook back and forth from her intense struggle with the lemon as she squeezed it with all her might.

BOOM!!

Out popped one drop of lemon juice!!!

The audience erupted in applause! The sounds of clapping, whistles and cheers rang throughout the fair. The strongman was blown away as he was compelled to show the audience the plate on which the drop of lemon juice had fallen. The old lady stood there onstage with her hands on her knees as she collected her breath. It was a scene to behold.

Then the strongman walked over with a check he had just written out for $1,000 and handed it to the lady as he said: "Ma'am, you have got to tell us. I've never had anyone squeeze an extra drop of juice out of that lemon. How did you do it?"

She replied: "Sir, I have to tell you. I am 74 years old. I just lost my husband. I've got three grandchildren that we're raising and I just lost my job. I needed that money."

The old lady was inspired. She was motivated. She had a reason WHY she needed to squeeze that juice out of the lemon. **With a big enough reason why, you will always find a way how.**

Your reason why is the fuel that burns the fire of inspiration and motivation inside of you.

So what is your "why"? Why do you do what you do? Why are you reading this right now? What do you want to accomplish in your life, this season, this week, today? What is your process for making those dreams a reality?

Most people think inspiration and motivation are things that you can do once in a while by reading a book, watching a movie or hearing a motivational speaker. Most people think that is all it takes for you to stay motivated. Realistically, that could not be farther from the truth. Although those experiences may spark a flame, in order to fan the flame and make it burn with a passion, you must have a BIG reason why.

MOTIVATION IS A DAILY DECISION

Imagine only brushing your teeth once a week. I hope, for everyone's sake, that you are disgusted by the thought of brushing your teeth only once a week! Your teeth would become yellow, feel hairy and would develop cavities and/or rot. In addition, nobody would want to hold a conversation with you because your breath would blow them away. My point is that you cannot brush your teeth once a week or take a bath once a week and expect your teeth to look good or you to smell good.

Inspiration and motivation work the same way as dental hygiene, except they are not for your oral health but for your mental performance health. You should mentally absorb some form of inspiration daily to motivate you in your preparation and performance. Do not read something inspiring once a week. Do not motivate yourself or your team once or even a couple of times a week. Inspiration and motivation must be performed every single day

THE DAILY DOMINATOR & SUCCESS HOTLINE

This is why I wrote the book *The Daily Dominator*. With The DOMINATOR you get to read one page a day of mental conditioning material, so that you can do a little a lot, not a lot a little, and maximize your mental game. Having everyone in your department and administrative team read the same page each day takes the guesswork out of having to create your own mental conditioning program. Your "do a little a lot" each day is already done; you just have to break it down with your team.

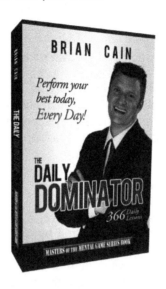

Dr. Rob Gilbert is a mentor of mine and master of the mental game and motivation. Dr. Gilbert is a professor of sports psychology at Montclair State University, and every morning at 7:30am EST he records a three-minute motivational message that you simply call and listen to. He has been doing this every day since January 22, 1992. He has recorded over 9,000 three-minute messages to date. Make this a part of your morning routine in order to start your day with a blast of positive energy. This has been one of the top contributing factors to my success over the past 10 years and my favorite part of my daily routine.

ADVERTISE TO YOURSELF

Have you ever wondered why companies are willing to pay three million dollars for a thirty-second commercial during the Super Bowl? The common response to this question is that tens of millions of people watch the Super Bowl. This is true, but the real reason that advertising works is that advertisements create lasting images within the mind, so that when people go out to consume products, those products from the advertisements jump to the front of their minds.

The same tactics of advertising apply to inspiring peak performance. Advertising to yourself will enhance your preparation and help create the mindset for success that you want. Similar to any successful marketing campaign, before creating sporadic marketing pitches, you must know what message you are wanting to send about your brand or product and the most effective methods for marketing that product.

KEVIN YOUNG – OLYMPIC ADVERTISING

The current world record holder in the 400-meter hurdles, with a time of 46.78 seconds, is the 1992 Summer Olympics gold medalist Kevin Young. When Young got to the Olympic Village in Barcelona, he advertised his Olympic goal to himself by writing it down, everywhere. When asked about his preparation in an interview after his world record performance, Young responded by saying, "My goal this year was to run 46.89. I wrote that everywhere in my room, even here up at the Village. I took a pencil and wrote it on the wall. I integrated it into a lot of things I do at home. I just got into the habit of writing the number around, everywhere I go."

Young used the power of self-advertising his goals by putting his goal in writing, where he could see it often for motivation. As an aspiring peak performer, you too should advertise your goals to yourself by putting them everywhere you can see them. If you truly desire something, you should be able to visualize it at every turn as you go through your day. Self-advertising helps you to focus on what you want, not on what you are trying to avoid.

CAIN'S COACHING POINT:
What goals can you write out and post around your office?

_____

_____

SIGNS OF SUCCESS

An excellent habit to develop is collecting inspirational phrases, pictures and images to create "signs of success" to hang around your living and office space. This provides you with visuals for motivation that you will see on a daily basis. When you see these signs of success every day, they become part of your everyday thought process. After a few days or a week seeing a particular sign, your goal will be to commit this sign of success to memory and, more importantly, to have it effectively motivate you to action.

Administrators most often self-advertise signs of success by hanging photos, quotes and other images all around their office and classroom. Pictures of those who inspire them, quotes that motivate them to continuously check in on their perspective, and mental conditioning statements such as **"Don't count the days, make the days count"** are reminders of the importance of today. Whenever you need them, these inspirational advertisements catch your eye and keep you inspired and motivated on your journey up the Mountain of Excellence.

The signs of success are simple ways to advertise the peak performance mentality and mental conditioning principles you want to adopt in your position and in life.

MAKE YOUR OWN SIGNS OF SUCCESS

Draw from the material and information you have acquired from this book and make your own signs of success. By creating your signs of success, you put your knowledge of peak performance to use and enhance the process of mentally conditioning the habit of excellence.

CAIN'S COACHING POINT:
Based on the content within this book, what are three captions for signs of success that you will hang in your office or classroom to stay inspired?

_____

_____

_____

EXAMPLES OF SELF-ADVERTISEMENT

Now that you know the importance of the signs of success and have created mental game marketing campaigns for yourself, let me share with you what other players have reported hanging in their rooms as signs of success. Remember, at all levels of competition, you are never too young, too old, too bad or too good to stay inspired.

1. A vision board collage of all your goals and what you want to accomplish.

2. A picture of a state championship stadium where that event will be held.

3. A poster of Muhammad Ali or other athletes who inspire the mentality that you want to develop.

4. A poster of your Championship Culture that will motivate you to continue to do the work necessary to live out your vision.

5. An inspirational quote from your favorite author.

BATHROOM MIRROR – DRY ERASE MARKER

Another great technique worth revisiting so you can stay inspired is to write your goals on your bathroom mirror with a dry erase marker. Whenever you enter the bathroom, you will see your goals and be reminded of the mindset you want to develop to become a peak performer. Essentially, your mirror becomes a goal-oriented sign of success.

I have worked with professional mixed martial arts fighters who, immediately upon arriving in Vegas at their hotel room, take out a dry erase marker and write their mental game reminders on the mirror. Writing on their mirror sets the tone for their peak performance mentality; whenever they enter the bathroom, they are reminded of their desired mindset and the need to focus on that mindset and process for performance excellence.

GOAL CARDS CARRIED ALL THE TIME

Another strategy you can use is to carry a card in your wallet with your personal goals displayed on it. Carrying a goal card will make you 35% more likely to make those goals come true because you have constant reinforcement whenever you open your wallet. Whenever you do open your wallet, take a look at that card and mentally check in with how you are moving forward to achieve your goals. This form of self-advertising will go wherever you go.

VISION BOARDS

One of the best motivational exercises you can do as an individual and as a team to help with inspiration and motivation is to create a vision board. A vision board is simply a collage of your goals and what you desire to accomplish. I strongly encourage you to create a vision board for yourself, and if you are on a team, I highly recommend you create one together as a team-building and team-focusing exercise.

You will never outperform your self-image. Making a vision board of images will inspire you to accomplish your goals. Place it where you will see it every day. This will keep your goals in the front of your mind and motivate you to achieve them. I personally started using vision boards in 2007, and annually revisit my own board the first week in July. Below is a picture of my personal vision board.

As you can see on my vision board, I want to speak in every state in the country. The ones that are white are the ones where I have not had a chance to speak YET. I want to help teams win national championships (accomplished in 2012, 2014 2X). I want to spend more time fishing and hiking in the mountains. I want to read at least one book every month. I want to be a better listener. I want to keep my weight under 200 pounds. I want to have better balance in my life between work and relaxation, and I want to live the core values of being positive, disciplined, progressive and committed to others. I also wanted to be a #1 Best-selling Author (which has been accomplished with my first book *Toilets, Bricks, Fish Hooks and PRIDE*).

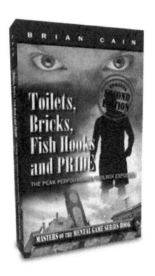

I keep my vision board with me in my binder, and I look at it multiple times each week. I have a copy of my vision board on my desk at home and on my desk at the office. The vision board serves as a reminder for me to constantly ask myself: *Is what I am working on right now helping me get to where I want to go?* The vision board is great for helping create the awareness you need to constantly check in on your progress towards achieving your goals, and to refocus yourself on what you want to accomplish.

WORK TO MAKE "IT" WORK

Here's the significant difference between peak performers and the rest of humanity: Peak performers understand that you must work to make "it" work. Whatever that "it" is, it's all about investing time and energy into a process of development that will make you excellent at what you do, and thus will bring you success. The vision board process has worked for me, it has worked for Jack Canfield (author of *Chicken Soup for the Soul*) as he talks about in the documentary *The Secret*, and it has worked for thousands of other people. It will work for you when you work it.

WATCH OUT FOR THE NEGAHOLICS

If you are an unenthusiastic, pessimistic cynic, often referred to as a "Donnie Downer" or a negaholic, and you believe that ***"This mental conditioning stuff is bogus, I just want to play"*** or ***"This stuff is never actually going to improve my performance,"*** well, you are right!

Whether you think you can or think you can't, you are right and you are stuck in the first two of the four stages of acceptance.

THE FOUR STAGES OF ACCEPTANCE

The four stages that we all go through to accept something new are as follows. Where are you?

1. This ain't for me.
2. This is OK for others.
3. I will try it.
4. I can't believe I did it any other way.

Everyone starts in stage one or two. If you have filled out the CAIN'S COACHING POINTS – actually filled them out with a pen in the book – then you are at stage three and will get to stage four.

The sad part about reality is that less than half the people who read this book will ever put pen to paper and answer the questions in the book. If that is you and you are reading this... STOP! Stop reading and start investing. If you want to truly be the best you can be, STOP. Go back and answer the questions in the book and then come back to this point.

If you actually did go back and answer the questions with pen to paper, my hat is off to you. You are pursuing excellence. If you did not and kept reading, so be it, your decision has been made. However, I invite you to get off the average train and head to station excellence.

There will be skeptics who think the mental game is a crutch or a magic pill. What the skeptics do not understand is that **you have to work to make it work.** The reason mental conditioning exercises will not work for them is a result of their refusal to try and make it work. It is not rocket science – if you do not attempt to make something work, of course it will not! It is the same logic as the old saying, "You miss 100 percent of the shots you do not take." You must believe in the benefits of mental conditioning for your performance to improve, and there are real, tangible payoffs.

The use of signs of success and vision boards will help you stay focused on your goals, and they will help you get motivated and stay inspired to DO THE WORK that it takes to be successful.

CAIN'S COACHING POINT:
If you noticed anyone on your team who has openly dismissed mental conditioning and stopped reading this book, reflect on how his attitude and actions affect the team. If his mentality is adversely affecting team chemistry, I'd suggest confronting that teammate or making your coach aware of the situation, as an expression of genuine concern for the well-being of the team throughout the season. Sometimes these moments can make all the difference in an athlete's career or even the person's life, because someone took the time and cared enough to step up, maybe more than that person cares about himself.

MOTIVATIONAL MOTION PICTURES

Motivational videos, inspirational movies, and highlight reels are another tremendous tool for peak performers. Similar to the video enhancement in mental imagery, there is no debating that watching some form of motivational motion picture or video before a practice or a game will inspire your performance on that day.

Watching a personal motivational video clip every morning as part of your morning routine also provides great reinforcement for the kind of person and player you want to be today. Regardless of how you feel when you wake up, the video clips you watch will get you fired up to DOMINATE that day and do the work necessary to advance further up the Mountain of Excellence.

CAIN'S GAME PLAN:
I challenge you to make your own personal highlight video. You can use footage of yourself or of others on YouTube to inspire your performance. Then watch this video on a routine basis.

INSPIRE YOUR DAILY DOMINATION

Whether you read a chapter in this book, watch an inspirational movie clip or use any number of the various methods for inspirational motivation, you must build motivation into your daily routine to become inspired to take action. You will have more success spending 3-5 minutes a day getting inspired and motivated than you will if you spend one hour once a week. Remember, if you get inspired a little a lot, you will have more success than if you get inspired a lot a little.

By the end of using this book, you will possess the information necessary to transform yourself into a peak performer. It is thus imperative that you motivate yourself to master the mental game in your daily preparation and performance ACTION, not just understand what you should do. Be the one who DOES IT!

Remember, intelligence is acting on the knowledge you have acquired. Use the strategies for motivation and inspiration from within this chapter to inspire your climb up to the summit of the Mountain of Excellence.

CHAPTER #10 REVIEW

- Have a big reason "why" and you will always find a way how.

- Make yourself inspired daily by reviewing motivational material.

- Advertise your goals to yourself.

- Make signs of success for motivation.

- Write daily goals on your mirror and make longer-term goal cards.

- Self-advertise during performance by writing on athletic tape.

- Create vision boards for performance goals.

- Work to make your goals a reality.

- Watch motivational video clips for inspiration.

- If you get inspired a little a lot, you will have more success than if you get inspired a lot a little.

CONCLUSION

PURSUING EXCELLENCE

> "Far and away the best prize that life has to offer is the chance to work hard at work worth doing."
>
> *Theodore Roosevelt*
> *26th President of the United States*

Excellence is being at your best when it means the most – every single moment and every single day.

This concept rules supreme in peak performance, transcending and penetrating all other aspects of mental conditioning. It is assuming personal responsibility in your daily pursuit of excellence that will make you a champion, because consistency of effort wins. Excellence is about the cultivation of superior mental strength through the process of establishing the proper routines, positive self-talk and an elite mindset, in preparation for inevitable battles through adversity in your leadership role and in life.

After all the mental conditioning material we have covered in this book, you should be both informed and well on your way to achieving your goal of performance excellence in athletic administration. We have outlined the fundamental principles of mental conditioning, and discussed how to adapt these principles and apply them on your journey to the summit of the Mountain of Excellence. This conclusion explains the purpose of necessary devotion to excellence within your daily performance.

EXCELLENCE IS A LIFESTYLE, NOT AN EVENT

Truly excellent individuals recognize that excellence is not something you do once in a while; you must strive to be excellent all the time – that is, twenty-four hours a day, seven days a week, and three hundred sixty-five days a year. Excellence is a stain you can't wipe off. I hope this book has stained you with excellence.

THREE DOORS & THE LAW OF AVERAGES

You have three doors you can choose to open. You can open the door called WIN, you can open the door called LOSE, or you can open the door called EXCELLENCE. The pursuit of excellence is about more than winning; performance excellence transcends winning. Excellence is a lifestyle; winning is an event that takes place at a moment in time.

Remember that the law of averages says that if you play your best, you give yourself the best chance to win, but you are not guaranteed to win. As a peak performer, you cannot control the outcome; all you can do is work the process to the best of your ability and give yourself the best opportunity for success on that day. The daily pursuit of excellence is the only way to get there.

> "Be miserable. Or motivate yourself. Whatever has to be done, it's always your choice."
>
> *Dr. Wayne Dyer*
> *Author & Motivational Speaker*

THE EXCELLENCE OF BLUE ANGELS

Excellence is about preparing more than other people are willing to, and working smarter than other people think is necessary. It is paying close attention to detail within the process in order to give

you the results you desire. The Blue Angels are a group of United States Navy Fighter Pilots that perform aerial shows all over the country. What their audiences witness is excellence in motion. What the audience does not see is that the entire performance process demands precision and a commitment to excellence before, and after, they take to the skies.

As some of the most dedicated and excellent performers on the planet, the Blue Angels use mental imagery, video analysis, and a routine brief and debriefing process. Each of these takes about twice as long as the flight itself to prepare for, and then learn from, each event they perform. The Blue Angels are known for their tight diamond formation in the air, where only 36 inches separate a plane from its wingtip to the canopy of the other planes (36 inches is about how far your head is from your feet when you sit down and read this). They perform aerial maneuvers at a speed of one mile every 9 seconds, or a closure rate, two planes flying directly towards each other at one mile every 4-½ seconds – almost 1,000 miles per hour. There is no room for error, and team excellence in their performance is critical.

PURSUIT OF EXCELLENCE OVER PERFECTION

The Blue Angels understand that their pursuit of excellence is different than the pursuit of perfection. They know that there has never been the perfect flight. They are constantly evaluating performance on video, looking for areas of improvement, paying close attention to the details of their flights, and even evaluating the way they march to their airplanes. The Blue Angels team is a model of excellence, and these pilots are truly dedicated to progress and making the team better in their pursuit of excellence TODAY!

When you see the Blue Angels or other peak performers, they make what they do look very easy, and we think they are gifted. Do not be fooled by their grace and proficient performance. Although they may appear to have been blessed with a few more gifts than Joe Normal, even they have climbed the Mountain of Excellence one step at a time, and they would be the first to tell you so.

A WORLD CHAMPION STATE OF MIND

Whether you have the physical talent of a world champion or not is irrelevant. Physical skill makes these champions visibly impressive, but more important is their mental toughness. The story behind their physical prowess is the story of their mental prowess – because it is their incredible work ethic, their capacity to embrace adversity, and their insatiable desire to improve to which they owe their success. One of the most beautiful aspects of the mental game is that, regardless of physical skill, you can become a master of the mental game.

Most people believe that you must be great before you can practice like the great ones. Well, most people have got it all wrong. Anyone can execute this program to cultivate the mindset of a champion. You may not have the same personality characteristics or natural energy flowing through your veins, but anyone can prepare with the same mental intensity as a world champion. The individual gifts and abilities are entirely dependent upon the person, but mental programs may be adopted universally so that you can be the best version of yourself at this given point in your life.

THE CLIMB IS THE DISCOVERY

As we have discussed throughout this manual, performance, in administration, in leadership and in life, is comparable to a journey up a mountain. The journey is yours and you alone have the ability to set the tone of your performance to conquer the climb. The mountain you set your sights on is your choice, and the journey is your discovery.

Each mountain you approach will require different physical skills that you must master, but the mental skill will remain the same. There will be some mountains that serve as pleasure climbs, while others will challenge your very existence by demanding every ounce of your physical and mental abilities. Sometimes you will be climbing a mountain and you will realize you no longer wish to reach the summit. Sometimes you will need to return to base camp, take a break, and return to conquer the summit at a later date. Each journey up a mountain is a journey of self-discovery, and through each experience you learn a little about yourself and a little bit about the journey. At the end of the day, it is the journey to the summit, not the summit itself, that makes reaching the summit worthwhile.

THE JOURNEY IS THE REWARD,
THE DESTINATION IS THE DISEASE

My hope is that, by the end of this book, you will have learned how to be an independent, peak performance mountaineer in your administrative role and in life – one who understands that although you may reach the summit of the mountain you are climbing, there is no summit in life and there is no summit to your excellence.

You are on a journey in which the journey is the reward and the destination is the disease. You must understand that every climb is a process and that proper preparation is imperative. You must create a mental road map, detailing where you want to go and who you must become to be worthy of reaching the summit. **Remember, if you want more, you must become more.**

Becoming more will give you the best chance to reach the summit of any mountain. Once you reach the summit and have thoroughly enjoyed the view, it is time to return to base camp and start climbing another.

CAIN'S COACHING POINT:
There will always be another mountain to climb. Throughout your journeys up the Mountains of Excellence, recognize that there is no final summit, there is no finish line. You are on a journey called life and your best bet is to DOMINATE THE DAY, every day, and enjoy this amazing ride.

SUCCESS = THE RESULT OF EXCELLENCE

I have said this before, and I will repeat myself for emphasis. There is no shortcut to performance excellence; there is no easy way to the summit of your mountain. *You don't get the same satisfaction from helicoptering to the summit as you do from climbing.*

Excellence is something you cannot purchase or be gifted, just as success is not something you simply randomly discover. Excellence is the result of a self-transformative journey to becoming more, a journey that you choose to actively endure. Once you develop a strict adherence to personal excellence, you are bound to discover the success you are looking for in *ALL ASPECTS OF YOUR LIFE!*

CREATE YOUR LEGACY

We are going to perform one final visualization exercise called "Fast Forward". This will help put you into a moment that you desire and one that you will create. Make this as realistic as possible so you can be in tune with the connection of your mind and heart.

We are going to "Fast Forward" to your retirement party. You have just completed your career in education and athletic administration. The celebration is in your honor. Imagine the venue where the party is held. Gaze around the room at the decorations and the layout of the space. Look at those in attendance. Hear the sounds of the music playing gently in the background. Take notice of the buzz in the conversations among those closest to you. Smell the food that will be served. Soak it all in, for this moment is about you and the sum of your todays – your career.

In the faint distance you hear the clinging of a glass with a fork, indicating that it is time for someone to speak. You notice that, over by the podium at the head of the room, are five people: your spouse, a former student-athlete, a member of the coaching staff, a member of the community, and your accountability partner. What do you want them to say about you?

Understand clearly that what you do each and every day matters, and you can create whatever message you want delivered by those who will speak on your behalf. You have an opportunity in this life to make a difference and be influential to the people around you. Do not ever lose sight of the fact that YOUR LIFE MATTERS! Every day is a gift, for you never know when your final curtain call will happen.

It is my hope that you embrace the role that you have been given. Sometimes people choose leadership and sometimes leadership chooses them. **Leadership has chosen you**. Make the most of your moments in order to best serve those around you and to leave your mark on this world that will be felt for generations to come.

CAIN'S COACHING POINT:
If you have found value in using this book, and if it has helped you in any way, consider giving a copy to five people whom you care about and want to see take their performance to the next level.

By giving this book to others, you are helping them find the ideas and mental keys that will unlock their potential.

You will help them live a more fulfilled and excellent journey as they climb their Mountain of Excellence. This book could

forever alter the course of someone's life. It could be you who provides the push as a great teammate. Without you, they might never even start hiking.

Write down five people to whom you wish to give a copy of this book:

1) _____

2) _____

3) _____

4) _____

5) _____

THE MENTAL CONDITIONS FOR EXCELLENCE

Through this book you have learned many mental conditioning strategies and peak performance principles to help you proceed on your journey to the summit of the Mountain of Excellence. Regardless of your position, the utilization of these mental conditioning principles and fundamentals are necessary to help achieve an elite and excellent performance state of mind.

At the conclusion of going through *The Mental Game of Athletic Administration,* you have learned how to:

• Live in the present moment and maximize your time;

• Act differently than how you feel and start having good bad days;

• Focus on the process over the outcome;

• Identify what you can control and what you cannot;

• Have your own personal philosophy and core values for life;

• Challenge your limiting beliefs and your perspective;

• Stay positive in the face of adversity;

• Develop preparation and performance routines for a consistently high-level performance;

• Take responsibility for your performance and life;

• Relax, recover and gain control of your thoughts, feelings and emotions;

• Recognize your signal lights and develop the awareness to win;

• Release negative thoughts and refocus back to the present when you get distracted;

• Move from intelligence and thinking to action and results;

• Use mental imagery to help you prepare and be more confident in your performance;

• Inspire and motivate yourself to make the impossible possible;

• Take action steps to make excellence a lifestyle, not an event.

Remember, you will reach the summit of the Mountain of Excellence by focusing on the next 200 feet. When you take Personal Responsibility In Daily Excellence, everything else will take care of itself. Today, sign your name with excellence on everything and everyone you touch, and I will see you at the summit!

YOUR SIGNATURE HERE   DATE

In Excellence,

Your Mental Conditioning Coach

Brian M. Cain

@BrianCainPeak
www.BrianCain.com

CONCLUSION REVIEW

- Excellence is being at your best when it means the most – every single day.

- Excellence is a lifestyle, not an event.

- You have three doors you can choose to open. You can open the door called WIN, you can open the door called LOSE, or you can open the door called EXCELLENCE.

- Excellence is about preparing more than other people are willing to, and working smarter than other people think is necessary.

- The pursuit of excellence is constructive; the pursuit of perfection will destroy you.

- Anyone can develop a world champion state of mind.

- The journey makes reaching the summit worthwhile.

- The journey is the reward and the destination is the disease.

- Success is the result of excellence.

- When you take PRIDE (Personal Responsibility In Daily Excellence) in your performance, everything else will take care of itself.

DOMINATE THE DAY!

ABOUT THE AUTHORS

WHO IS BRIAN M. CAIN?

Brian M. Cain, MS, CMAA, is a former high school athletic director and one of the youngest AD's to ever have earned the prestigious NIAAA CMAA designation. Cain is also a #1 best-selling author, speaker, trainer and expert in the fields of Sport Psychology and Peak Performance. He has worked with coaches, athletes and teams at the Olympic level and in the National Football League (NFL), National Basketball Association (NBA), National Hockey League (NHL), Ultimate Fighting Championship (UFC), and Major League Baseball (MLB).

Cain is high school athletic directors premier mental conditioning coach, and has worked with more AD's teams and athletes than anyone else in the area of peak performance coaching. He is the trusted authority and expert that coaches, players and parents turn to when they want to take the mental game to the next level.

Some of the athletic programs around the country he has worked with include the University of Alabama, Auburn University, Florida State University, the University of Iowa, the University of Maryland, the University of Mississippi, Yale University, The University of Notre Dame and many more.

He has delivered his award-winning seminars and presentations at coaches' clinics, leadership summits and athletic directors' conventions all over the country.

Please visit www.BrianCain.com/Monday to sign up for his weekly newsletter. Visit www.BrianCain.com/Calendar to see when Cain will be in your area so you can experience the benefits of having him come in and work with your team.

ABOUT THE AUTHORS

WHO IS ETHAN MILLER?

Ethan Miller is currently the Athletic Director at Central Springs High School in Manly, IA. Along with his duties as AD, he teaches courses in Character & Leadership, Health and Physical Education. He is still very involved in coaching, serving as the Head Baseball Coach and Assistant Girls Track & Field Coach.

Ethan garnered All-American honors playing baseball at Northwestern College in Orange City, IA and was recently inducted into the Northwestern College Athletic Hall of Fame. He has a bachelor's degree in Physical Education and a master's degree in Sports Management.

Ethan brings his knowledge and experiences in peak performance to *The Mental Game for Athletic Administration*. He adds a tremendous perspective gained throughout his time as a leader in educational athletics. Ethan provides strategies to maximize daily performance, enhance the culture within schools and master the mental game of administration.

He and his wife Becky, who teaches science in the Central Springs District and is the Head Girls Track & Field Coach, reside in Mason City, IA with their daughter Gretta. You can connect with Ethan on Twitter @BandEMiller!

CONNECT WITH CAIN ON SOCIAL MEDIA

 @BrianCainPeak

 /BrianCainPeak

 /BrianCainPeak

 /BrianCainPeak

 @BrianCainPeak

 @BrianCainPeak

WHERE'S CAIN?

Find out when Brian will be in your area and inquire about having him come educate, energize, and empower you and your team or organization!

View Cain's Calendar at

BrianCain.com/Calendar

Contact Cain by visiting

BrianCain.com/Contact

MONDAY MESSAGE

Want to receive tips, techniques, strategies and stories to help you close the gap from where you are to where you want to be?

Get Cain's Monday Message delivered directly to your Inbox each week!

Join now at

BrianCain.com/Monday

"We review the Monday Message every week as part of our weekly routine and mindset management. It has served as a great resource for our staff and players and keeps Cain's system in the forefront of their minds."

Tony Reno
Head Football Coach
Yale University

PODCAST

Every Wednesday, Cain takes you inside the locker rooms, coaches' offices and meeting rooms of the best teams in the country. Learn how the best of the best use this program to maximize their potential in their life and competitive arena.

Subscribe on iTunes now at

BrianCain.com/Podcast

View Archives at

BrianCain.com/Blog

PRODUCTS

Brian Cain is a #1 best-selling author of more than 30 books and training programs that are being used by Champions around the world.

If you're looking for the best of the best when it comes to Mental Conditioning, Performance Psychology, Organizational Leadership, Team Building and Character Education, look no further. Cain's world-class product selection will help you maximize your potential and become a Master of the Mental Game.

View all of Cain's Products at

BrianCain.com/Products

LIVE EVENTS

THE

BRIAN CAIN

Want to master the 12 Pillars of Peak Performance in your life? Get your total immersion learning experience by attending Cain's next live 2-day event.

Reserve your spot now at

BrianCain.com/Experience

Go deep inside 1 of the 12 Pillars of Peak Performance by attending Cain's next live 1-day Bootcamp.

Reserve your spot now at

BrianCain.com/Bootcamp

INNER CIRCLE

Want to be the best? Surround yourself with like-minded individuals who are on the same mission as you by joining Cain's Inner Circle. As an Inner Circle member, you'll receive:

- Monthly Audio & Corresponding Newsletter
- Weekly Monday Message Worksheets
- Exclusive Access to Private Facebook Group
- Reserved Inner Circle Seating at Live Events
- and much more...

Join today by visiting

BrianCain.com/InnerCircle

> "You become the average of the 5 people you surround yourself with most."
>
> **Brian Cain**

KEYNOTE SPEAKING

Cain has spoken on stages all over the world and delivers *The 12 Pillars of Peak Performance* at retreats, clinics, leadership summits, and conventions. Cain will inform, inspire and give you the proven strategies and systems necessary to get the most out of your career and life.

Book Cain to speak at your next event!

BrianCain.com/Speaking

TEAM CONSULTING

Brian Cain is the coach that top university and high school athletic teams turn to for a competitive advantage. He works with you to customize *The 12 Pillars of Peak Performance* to help your program maximize your athletes' potential. There are a limited number of slots available each year.

Get started by visiting

BrianCain.com/Consulting

1-ON-1 COACHING

Cain works one-on-one with athletes and coaches of all levels. He is now offering one-on-one coaching opportunities where he can work with you directly to apply the information in this manual to your life so that you can compete at the highest level and win the game of your life. This is the **most exclusive access** to Cain and there are a limited number of spots available.

Get started today by visiting

BrianCain.com/Coaching